THE EMMANUEL COLLEGE GUIDE TO CAREERS IN MARKETING

Discover and Land Your Perfect Digital Marketing Job

TABLE OF CONTENTS

I. INTRODUCTION

The world of business is rapidly transforming, driven by new consumer expectations, globalization, and technology. The Emmanuel College School of Business & Management believes that success in today's business world requires embracing and shaping these dynamics to create both social and economic value. That's why for over (x) years, our commitment to excellence has prepared students to become socially responsible leaders, innovative thinkers, and ethical decision-makers.

No profession has been more impacted by the forces of transformation than marketing. The proliferation of data, digital platforms, and artificial intelligence has enabled companies to reach, engage, and understand their customers in radically new ways. These new capabilities have radically reshaped existing marketing roles, and created a vast number of new, and highly specialized ones.

The purpose of this book is to help students and career-switchers understand this new and complex landscape. Ultimately, The Emmanuel Guide to Careers in Marketing hopes to provide you with a resource that assists you in finding a happy, satisfying, and rewarding career.

This book includes several valuable resources. One section addresses the 'basics' of marketing: "What is marketing?', "What do marketers do?, and 'What are career options in marketing?', and 'Where is marketing going?. Another section provides an overview of the dynamic world of digital marketing and provides insights into the most promising marketing career paths, and the essential skills and capabilities required for future success.

Also included is a step by step 'playbook' guiding you to that 'perfect job':

• PLAY #1: Capture Insights, which provides guidance and tools enabling you to assess your life goals & career interests.

• PLAY #2: Develop A Career Strategy, will help you create a 'short list' of marketing and digital marketing career opportunities that best meet your goals and interests.

• PLAY #3: Execute The Strategy, which provides detailed profiles of dozens of marketing roles, along with advice on how to land that first job.

• PLAY #4: Optimize Career Potential, serves as a guide to ensuring you remain 'relevant' and maximize your long-term career potential.

Last but not least, the final section provides a comprehensive description of dozens of marketing, and digital marketing career options, with a particular focus on the 'hottest' jobs today and the top 'trending' jobs of the future.

Just as the Emmanuel College School of Business prepares students to compete in today's dynamic business work, we hope this book will help guide you to a successful and rewarding career.

Sincerely,

Anne Marie Pasquale, Esq.

Dean, Emmanuel College School of Business & Management

II. WHAT IS MARKETING?

There are dozens of definitions of Marketing, and if you read them all you'll still struggle to understand what it means. Part of the problem is that marketers (myself included) like to make things much more complicated than they are (must be a form of job security I guess…).

I find that Phillip Kotler's definition best captures the essence of marketing: 'the science and art of exploring, creating, and delivering value to satisfy the needs of a target market at a profit. In somewhat simpler terms, marketing is about developing and selling products that customers want - and are willing to pay extra for, and want to buy over and over again It's a systematic approach to uncovering the unmet needs of the customer and then designing and selling a product or service that satisfies these needs.

With innovation and strategy at the 'core', there are four primary activities of the Marketer:
· Capturing Market and Customer Insights
· Developing The Marketing Strategy
· Executing The Marketing Strategy
·Measuring and Continually Optimizing the Performance of the Marketing Plan

Each of these activities is highly specialized and requires distinct skills and capabilities leading to vastly different marketing career opportunities.

CAPTURING MARKET AND CUSTOMER INSIGHTS

Capturing market and customer insights is often called 'market research'. However, this term does not do justice to the important work done by market research professionals who convert data and information into valuable (and ideally unique) insights. This is the 'art and science' of understanding consumers and the business situation and why great market researchers are worth their weight in gold.

While the core responsibilities of the market researcher have not changed with the rise of digital and technology, the tools at their disposal certainly have. It's safe to say that ALL roles in this field are 'digital roles. *See Section V of the book for detailed descriptions of the hottest jobs: Market Research Manager and User Experience & Design Researcher.*

DEVELOPING THE MARKETING STRATEGY

All marketing roles require a degree of 'Strategy' but for simplicity, this book uses three broad categories: **Marketing Strategy, Corporate Brand Strategy, and Marketing Campaign Strategy.**

Marketing Strategy

No business will survive without a strategy that serves the needs of the customer in a way that sets it apart (differentiates it) from the competition. The Marketing Strategy is at the heart of any business plan and addresses two 'live or perish' questions for a business:

Which customers will I serve and how will we create value for

them?

No brand can serve all consumers. 'Consumers' defines a large group of potential buyers for a product. However, consumers consist of people with many different backgrounds, family situations, incomes, interests, and most importantly, 'needs'. A marketer who tries to create a one-size-fits-all product is doomed to a 'one size fits no one' failure. Therefore, the first step in developing a marketing strategy is to determine how consumers in a given market vary from one another. This is called 'segmentation', an analysis that divides the market into smaller clusters of customers that share similar attitudes, demographics, interests, and other factors.

With the segmentation, the business then needs to select the target audience. This means deciding which consumer cluster it believes provides the greatest business opportunity. Which cluster are my product's benefits most suited for? Are there enough consumers in this cluster to generate adequate revenue? Does the cluster have long-term growth potential? Etc.

How will deliver value to the target market and differentiate our product from competitors?

The heart of the marketing strategy answers the question 'why should I buy your product instead of other products on the market? The marketer must determine what uniquely differentiates their product to make it desirable, versus all others, by the target audience. This can take the form of functional and/or emotional differentiation. 'Functional differentiators' are tangible characteristics that make the product stand out. A higher quality product, a greater number of product features, or a lower price are examples of functional differentiators. 'Emotional differentiation' are intangible characteristics that serves the psychological needs of a customer. A product that provides the consumer with a sense of prestige, safety, or belonging are examples of emotional differentiators.

The final component of a marketing strategy is Positioning the product (the brand) in the mind of the target audience. Positioning in the essence of marketing communication and seeks to establish a unique 'mental space' among consumers for the brand name and its differentiators.

EXECUTING THE MARKETING STRATEGY

With the a strategy developed, the marketer is now ready to develop the marketing program consisting of the 'The 4P's'.

Product: What specific product(s) will we sell? In what varieties? What is the brand name and branding strategy? What type of packaging and with what design?

Place: Where will we sell it? In physical stores, online, or both? In department stores, convenience stores, supermarkets, etc.? Through a middleman or direct-to-the-consumer?

Price: At what price will we sell the product?' At a premium price to competitors, at the same price, or at a lower price?

Promotion: What is the marketing campaign strategy? How will consumers be aware of the brand? What's the best promotion mix to influence consumers to try the brand? Should we invest in digital media, search marketing, advertising, promotions, social media, event marketing, etc.?

Product management and Brand Management roles have overall responsibility for developing and executing the marketing strategy. Section V of the book provides detailed job descriptions of these functions and also highlights the nuances between 'Product Management', 'Digital Product Management', and 'Brand

Management'.

Marketing Campaign Strategy

The majority of marketing jobs are specialized roles focused on specific parts of the marketing campaign e.g. advertising, social media, the website, and promotional programs etc. But a single person or team creates the overall marketing campaign strategy towards the goal of delivering an 'integrated' program whereby each communication and promotion activity work synergistically to establish customer awareness o, and demand for the product.

Marketing (and digital) campaign strategy involves determining:
- The Campaign Target Audience – although the overall target market has been defined in the marketing strategy, the campaign strategy needs greater specificity i.e. is the campaign intended for subsegments such as specific geographies or ethnic groups? Will the campaign target new customers, existing customers or competitive users, etc.?
- The 'Objective' – what is the specific goal of the campaign? To create brand awareness? Stimulate trial or purchase? Drive brand loyalty?
- The Campaign 'Mix' – which marketing activities are most appropriate to reach and influence the target audience? During which weeks of the year?
- The 'Message' – what advertising and promotional messages will 'connect' with, and influence the target audience?

The Marketing Funnel

Campaigns generally fall into two categories: those intended to acquire a new customer and those intended to retain existing customers. So the campaign needs to be very clear about its purpose. The Marketing Funnel is a planning framework used by all marketers to define the primary objective of a campaign. There are several variations of the Funnel but I'll reference a four-stage Funnel consisting of the Awareness, Consideration, Acquisition, and Retention stages.

Awareness and Consideration (The 'Top Of The Funnel')
The 'Top of the Funnel' focuses on finding potential buyers and building awareness that the brand exists. Once this is established, the marketer then explains what the brand offers and why the customer should 'consider' buying it and focuses on clearly communicating the brand's key product benefits and features. Marketing roles at the top of the Funnel include advertising, media, social media, and web communications.

Acquisition (The 'Middle of the Funnel')
The 'Middle of the Funnel' is sometimes referred to as the 'Trial' or 'Acquisition' stage. Assuming your prospective customer is aware of your product, and considering buying it, the objective here is to prompt 'action' by the target audience that directly or indirectly leads to a sale. Marketing communication professionals who work at this stage implement a variety of programs to motivate prospects to sample a product, use a coupon, call the sales center, or request more product information. Expertise in this area is called Demand or Lead Generation and is one of the hottest areas of marketing now and has been revolutionized by digital media and technologies.

Retention (The 'Bottom of the Funnel'
The "Bottom of the Funnel" is referred to as "Retention" and focuses on maintaining an active and 'loyal' customer base. As we'll discuss, it is much more profitable for a brand to maintain a loyal customer than it is to find a new one. This book will review "Customer Relationship Management", another hot career track with excellent future potential.

Section II outlines campaign planning careers including Marketing

& Digital Campaign Managers, as well as 'Demand Generation' or 'Lead Generation' Managers.

MARKETING EXECUTION

Once the campaign strategy is determined, there are many specialized roles required to bring it to market. These are critical roles responsible for creating what the customer will see and 'experience' about the brand in advertising, online, and at the point of sale.

Section V of the book provides detailed descriptions of the roles within seven different types of Marketing Execution activities:
- Advertising & Media Management
- Social Media Management
- User Experience and Design
- Content Marketing
- Web Communication
- Search Engine Marketing
- Promotion Management

ANALYTICS AND OPTIMIZATION

Once the campaign is executed, it is essential to continually analyze how it's performing and what can be done to improve performance – and thus maximize campaign return on investment (ROI). By their actions and inactions, consumers provide marketers with massive amounts of data when engaging with the brand's advertising, social media posts, website, e-mail content, etc. Hidden in these data are the clues for optimizing campaign performance. Which elements of the campaign are working best to capture customer leads? Is Facebook advertising a better investment than Google AdWords? Is the brand priced for maximum sales and profit? Is it easy for web visitors to navigate the site? etc.

This is a highly specialized area and represents one of the hottest areas of digital marketing with Digital Analysts and Data Scientists in great demand. Please reference Section V of the book for detailed job descriptions.

III. The Age of Digital Marketing

Digital has changed nothing and EVERYTHING about marketing.

The core principles of marketing, Insights. Strategy, Execution, and Analytics remain the same and there is no '5th P' because of digital. Yet every aspect of these principles has been radically altered due to digital data, media, and technology. Since the introduction of 'digital' into the marketing lexicon, progressive marketers have embraced the potential of digital data and technology by asking themselves:

- How can digital assist me in creating deeper, faster, and more accurate market & customer insights?
- How can digital data and technologies create enhanced value for customers via new products, services, and solutions?
- How can digital technologies expand the distribution of

my product, making it more convenient for customers to buy it?

- How, can digital media create richer advertising and promotional experiences for my customer and enhance the image of my brand?
- How can massive amounts of data enable me to uncover unique insights to optimize the performance of my campaigns and do so quickly and on an ongoing basis?

Even prior to the pandemic, companies were increasingly transforming their marketing departments by investing in more staff, digital advertising, social media, and digital product development. However, the pandemic greatly accelerated the pace of this 'digital transformation'.

McKinsey's 2021 'The Future of Work' notes, '*The world of work is changing. Artificial intelligence and automation will make this shift as significant as the mechanization in prior generations of agriculture and manufacturing. While some jobs will be lost, and many others created, almost all will change. If you look at where the biggest gaps are, the top of the list are digital skills. (McKinsey Global Work Survey 2021).*

Another report noted, 'Building a core of top talent in priority areas, such as open-source developers, product owners, data engineers, cloud developers, and UX/UI designers, can be one of the most effective actions a company can take to accelerate its digital aspirations'.

Also, a recent LinkedIn report noted 400,000 marketing job openings with specialized digital roles accounting for half of them—a 33% increase versus the prior year. Also noted was a trend towards more flexibility in the hiring process as companies are more willing to hire remote workers and take on interns and contractors to fill talent gaps.

The bottom line is that digital marketing jobs, including entry-level ones, have never been in more demand. CCompanies are investing in, and competing for digital talent to accelerate business performance for several reasons:

· To capture market and customer insights
· To provide customers with a better digital experience
· To fuel digital innovation
· To acquire and retain new customers
· To maximize marketing campaign performance
· To become a more 'agile' and responsive businesses
· To expand to new channels of distribution

All the digital roles outlined in Section V of the book are 'in demand'. However, the following list represents the **HOTTEST JOBS** which will likely see significant future job growth and offer excellent pay:

Digital Marketing Specialists
- Digital Campaign Management
- Social Media Management
- Search Marketing Management

User Experience and Content Marketing
- User Experience Designer
- Interface Design
- User Experience Research
- Content Marketing Manager

Marketing Technology
- Marketing Technology Management

Data Analytics
- Marketing Analytics Manager
- Data Scientist

IV. THE PLAYBOOK

The purpose of this section is to guide you through a series of assessments that will ultimately provide you with a personalized 'short list' of potential marketing careers. The playbook consists of four 'Plays. These will seem familiar to you since it's based on the 'key marketing activities framework' we previously reviewed: Insights – Strategy – Execution – Optimization. Why does a marketing framework make sense for a career playbook?

Your search for the right digital career must begin with **Capturing Insights**, about your life goals, interests, and passions as well as insights into the tangible and intangible aspects of different career paths. You will need to define a **Career Path Strategy** that narrows down your 'Short List' of Career Options. Of course, the toughest task ahead of you is to land that ideal job. Having a detailed **Execution Plan** will maximize your chances of

getting hired. Finally, when you land that first job, the journey has just begun!

The phrase 'change is the only constant' completely defines the digital marketing career path. You will need to relentlessly learn and stay relevant to **'Optimize'** your career path trajectory.

PLAY #1: INSIGHTS

WHAT ARE YOUR LIFE AND CAREER ASPIRATIONS?

Before considering marketing as a career, I would strongly suggest first 'knowing thyself'. Career options are abundant with many variables that impact the right 'fit' for you. So, performing an honest self-assessment, that deeply considers your life goals, interests, passions, skills, and capabilities is VERY important.

Career Assessment Tools

If you are currently in school, take advantage of their career counseling resources and meet with your guidance counselor for one-on-one advice. If you are not in school, there are free online assessment tools you can use. These will ask you a battery of questions related to your values, skills, interests, personality, and motivations. Based on your responses, you'll receive career recommendations that most closely 'fit' with your profile.

I've taken the Myers-Briggs assessment (https://www.themyersbriggs.com/en-US/Products-and-Services/Myers-Briggs). Other well-known career assessment tools include:

· Mynextmove.org
· Myplan.com
· MAPP (assessment.com)
· Holland Code Career Test
· iSeek Clusters

I'd suggest taking several of these assessments and comparing the results. When taking the assessment, it's essential that you 'summon your innermost self' and honestly answer each question. Your answers should reflect 'Who You Are' and NOT 'The Person You Would Like to Be'. This is not at all saying you can't grow to become that person—but that comes later. You want the assessment to suggest a handful of career options that help point your career compass, and steer you away from career paths that you'll never enjoy.

In addition to the personal these assessments, the following section provides some additional things for you to consider.

WHAT INDUSTRY BEST ALIGNS WITH YOUR PERSONAL GOALS?

It's important to consider the pros and cons of different types of industries. The ideal industry for me serves humanity, brings rapid innovation to the market, is highly creative, is high-paying, is on the cutting-edge of 'cool',

and is known for a culture of caring and collaboration. Unfortunately, such an industry simply does not exist.

Often the most 'exciting' industries (music, TV, movies, etc.) look great from a distance but often the day-to-day job tasks can be boring and repetitive with an office culture that can be one of back-stabbing and 'phoniness'. I spent 3 years in the radio industry working with some truly talented and amazing colleagues. However, I witnessed jaw-dropping unprofessional behavior that killed my interest in the entertainment industry. As I discuss career options with young people today, I am truly impressed that their primary criteria for determining a career path is to serve a 'higher purpose'. Many industries enable this including healthcare, not-for-profit organizations, the fine arts, and teaching.

While marketing is an important function in all companies, its prominence and 'stature' can vary significantly depending on the industry. So, once you've decided that marketing is the best career path, you need to reflect on several important questions related to the industry:
· Is it important for marketing be the 'driver' of the business versus simply a secondary 'support' function?
· Is it important that the industry serve a 'higher purpose' and contributes to the betterment of humanity?
· How progressive and advanced is the marketing function within the industry? Will you learn leading-edge marketing skills?
· Does the industry have long-term growth potential?

· Does the industry invest heavily in marketing programs, ot just nominally?
· Last but not least, do you have a personal passion for the products or services created within the industry?

I asked myself three questions to determine whether or not an industry was right for me:

· Did it align with my **Personal Passions**.
· Did it serve a **'Higher Purpose'**.
· Would it provide me with a **Rewarding Career Experience** and enable me to continuously grow as a professional.

These three variables can often be at odds with one another. There is no better industry to develop advanced marketing skills than Consumer Packaged Goods. You'll be at the 'center of the action' and (at a young age) have responsibility for managing multimillion-dollar marketing budgets. But dedicating your life to marketing products found on grocery store shelves might not register high on your 'higher purpose' scale. Conversely, working in Life Sciences (healthcare-related industries) is all about saving and improving the lives of patients – the most noble of all industries. However, this is a sales and R&D-driven industry with marketing playing a necessary but 'supporting role'.

Of course, no one should be dissuaded to choose an industry based on their personal passions and interests. But as you begin your marketing career, you should consider if you will receive the marketing training you need

to remain competitive in future years. If your passion is automobiles or computers, then no worries…. All the major car and computer companies are great and sophisticated marketers. Beginning your career in other industries lacking sophisticated marketing departments will likely limit your ability to develop advanced marketing skills.

My recommendation is to first join a company that provides new hires with advanced marketing (and digital marketing) training. With these skills under your belt, you will be in a great position to pivot to an industry or company that you find personally more rewarding at some point in the future. Your skills will be transferable and 'in-demand', and ultimately enable you to have greater long-term career success.

In hindsight, I seemed to have taken my advice. I began my

career with Unilever working on such non-essential products as pasta sauce and margarine but received unmatched training in all aspects of marketing. I then pivoted to digital marketing and applied these skills within the technology (IBM), entertainment (Clear Channel), consumer goods (Samsung electronics), and life sciences (Boston Scientific) industries.

The following provides my thoughts on the career pros and cons of the industries I've worked in.

Consumer Packaged Goods (CPG) Industry

Pros

- CPG companies, e.g. Proctor & Gamble, generally have the most sophisticated marketing organizations and training programs. This is because company success is largely dependent on the ability of marketing to introduce innovative products and to execute effective advertising and promotion.
- Investment in marketing programs is significant – usually 6% - 10% of total company sales revenue.
- The marketing 'mix' is comprehensive and you will have hands-on exposure to advertising, digital, social media, web, mobile, and other marketing tactics.
- The pay is very good.

Cons

- CPG products tend to be mundane household staples – the types of products sold in grocery and drug stores.
- Most consumer packaged goods products compete in low, or no growth categories with intense competition.
- Competition for promotions is intense.

The Technology Industry

Pros

- Technology is a fascinating and dynamic industry driving

unprecedented advancements in all aspects of society - how we live, work, communicate, travel, play, learn, etc.
-    The industry will remain the drive of world economic growth and job creation.

Cons
-    Tech companies are driven by Engineering and Sales organizations with marketing playing a supporting role. Marketing has limited influence on what products are sold i.e. product innovation. Tech marketers focus largely on supporting the sales organizations and developing advertising and promotion.

Life Sciences Industries
Pros
-    You will be working in an industry with an unmatched 'greater purpose'—to improve health and save lives.
-    The people in this industry are the most sincere, respectful, and caring co-workers I have experienced.

Cons
-    Life Science companies, such as medical devices, are an Engineering and Sales-driven industry.
-    Except for pharmaceuticals, marketing within life sciences companies has been rather underdeveloped and generally served as a support function for sales (organizing sales events, creating trade brochures, etc.).
-    Marketing budgets are modest.

A COMPANY CULTURE THAT'S RIGHT FOR YOU
When choosing a specific company to work for, there are several factors to consider:

- Is the company healthy and growing (usually driven by its commitment to research and development)?
- What's the company 'culture' and does this align with your values and beliefs?
- What do current employees say about working there?
- Does the company promote from within, or are external people recruited for the most senior-level jobs?

It's also important to consider the company's 'mindset' related to the importance of marketing and digital marketing. The top brass in many companies grew up in a sales-driven and analog world. While many have embraced the importance of marketing and digital marketing, some remain unable to shed their old-fashioned mindset despite overwhelming evidence of the importance of modern marketing practices.

So, as you interview with different companies, assess their 'digital mindset'.

I worked at IBM during the first wave of digital. Unfortunately, many of my marketing colleagues simply could not expand their thinking beyond traditional advertising. Astonishingly, the Integrated Marketing Communications department did not consider web, e-mail marketing, and search marketing as their responsibility. While there were indeed several progressive thinkers and exceptions to this mindset, it all starts with the direction (or lack thereof) set by the CMO and other senior marketing executives.

PLAY # 2: DEVELOPING A CAREER STRATEGY
(Creating your 'Short List' of career options.)

Interests & Skills Matrix

The Interest & Skills Matrix maps marketing jobs within one of four quadrants based on two dimensions:

- 'Analytically' focused jobs versus 'Creative' focused jobs.
- 'Generalist' roles versus 'Specialist' roles

This matrix provides a good starting point to develop your career strategy by reflecting on these questions:

- Are you a 'numbers person' ('quantitative'), or a 'creative' person?
- Are you a 'strategist' (or better at 'specialized' activities?
- Are you relentlessly inquisitive ('discovery') or a person who's good at organizing projects and/or leading people?
- What's more interesting to you, 'running a 'business' or pursuing a very specialized role?

I **Interests & Skills Matrix**

Quadrant I - Generalist / Business Strategy	Quadrant II - Generalist / Creative & Discovery
✓ Product & Brand Management	✓ Brand Strategist
✓ Marketing Campaign Management	✓ Advertising Management
	✓ User Experience Research

<table>
<tr>
<td>

✓ Digital Marketing Management

</td>
<td></td>
</tr>
<tr>
<td>

Quadrant III - Specialist / Business Strategy

✓ (Digital) Data Analytics
✓ Data Scientist
✓ E-Commerce Management
✓ Digital Media Management
✓ Paid Search Management
✓ Social Media Ad Management
✓ Search Engine Optimization
✓ Marketing Automation Management
✓ Shopper Marketing
✓ Trade Marketing

</td>
<td>

Quadrant IV - Specialist / Creative & Discovery

✓ Market Research Management
✓ Website Communications Management
✓ Social Media Management
✓ Event Management
✓ Consumer Promotion Management
✓ Content Marketing
✓ User Experience Design
✓ Copy Writing
✓ (Digital) Graphic Design
✓ Digital Producer

</td>
</tr>
</table>

Quadrant I: Generalist / Business Strategy

Roles in this quadrant lead business and/or marketing campaign strategy. Product Management, Brand Management, Marketing Campaign Management, e-commerce, and Digital Marketing Management are all roles that 'play point' in deciding and managing the overarching strategy, business plan, and operating budgets. These are also 'leadership' roles, responsible for managing the people who will execute the marketing program. Career success factors include Analytical thinking, Leadership acumen, Project management, Strategic thinking, Financial acumen

These roles are grounded in 'data' and analysis, so strong quantitative skills are essential. They also require strong communication and influencing skills to gain the buy-in of senior management and other parts of the organization such as Sales and Finance.

Pros:
- Highest salary of all marketing roles
- Significant responsibility and visibility within the organization
- A pathway to executive management (in many, but not all industries)
- A variety of work activities with 'no two days the same
- Significant status within the organization
- Satisfaction of working with a wide variety of people
- Satisfaction of leading people

Cons:
- Heavy workload
- Stressful (most of the time)

- Less job security
- Office politics is 'par for the course'
- Fierce competition for promotions

Quadrant II: Generalist / Creative & Discovery

Roles in this quadrant lead important strategic work related to brand development, advertising, and digital design strategy. Key roles include Brand Strategy, Advertising Management, and User Experience Design Research.

Each of these are high-paying jobs requiring a combination of skills:
- deep expertise in branding, advertising, or user experience design
- the ability to think 'conceptually'
- strong verbal and written communication skills
- the ability to lead and manage people

Pros:
- High salaries
- Fairly stable job security

- Satisfaction of having your work seen by many people
- An ability to deliver 'breakthrough' marketing results
- Satisfaction of working with a wide variety of people

Cons
- Stressful (some of the time)
- Somewhat less job security
- Not a pathway to executive management
- Many 'cooks in your kitchen' evaluating your work
- Limited opportunity to work remotely

Quadrant III: Specialist / Business Strategy

Roles in this quadrant focus on a variety of important quantitative and specialized marketing activities. Key areas include management of Data Science, Data Analytics, Marketing Automation, Digital Media, Search Marketing, and Market Research.

Each role requires strong quantitative skills, a keen understanding of digital technology, and the ability to draw actionable conclusions from data. Solid presentation skills are also needed to clearly communicate recommendations across all levels of the organization.

Pros
- Good to very high pay (Data Science)
- High job security
- Limited office politics
- Cutting-edge work with strong potential to impact the business
- Satisfaction of being an important and respected member of the team
- Significant opportunity to work remotely

Cons
- Stressful at times

- Limited paths for career advancement
- Not a pathway to executive management
- Less day-to-day interaction with other people in the organization

Quadrant IV: Specialist / Creative & Discovery

Roles in this quadrant focus on executing highly specialized marketing and digital marketing activities. These jobs create the designs, words, and images that 'bring to life' how the customer experiences the brand across advertising and digital channels.

Website Communication, Content Marketing, User Experience & Interaction Design, Social Media, Copywriting, and Digital Production jobs require a high degree of training to master specialized skills in addition to having Tech-savvy, Organization and Project management, Communication, Strategic thinking, and Business creativity capabilities.

Pros
- Good to very high pay
- High job security
- Limited office politics
- Creative work is seen by many
- Satisfaction of being an important and respected member of the team
- Significant opportunity to work remotely

Cons
- Stressful at times
- Limited paths for career advancement
- Not a pathway to executive management
- Less day-to-day interaction with other people in the organization

I'd suggest reviewing some job satisfaction surveys that you can

find online including these two on glassdoor.com:
- https://www.glassdoor.com/blog/jobs-highest-satisfaction-2019/
- https://www.glassdoor.com/List/Best-Jobs-in-America-LST_KQ0,20.htm

You'll notice many of the roles mentioned in our 'matrix' including product marketing, UX designer, brand manager, data scientist, communications manager, and marketing manager.

Creating Your CAREER SHORTLIST

First, write down the five to seven most important things you are looking for in a career e.g.:
- a high salary
- the ability to work remotely
- a desire for rapid advancement
- a job that is creative, etc.

Second, reference Section II of this book and read the general descriptions provided for each area of marketing: Insights, Strategy, Execution, and Measurement & Optimization.

Third, read each of the detailed job descriptions within those areas of marketing that seem 'interesting' and that have the potential to meet your career interests.

Fourth, for each detailed job description that you like, use a scale from one to ten to rank each job against your most important criteria. A '10' would indicate a job criteria that is extremely important to you while a '1' would indicate that the criteria is not very important.

Fifth, then total up the scores for each to see which job ranks highest 'all things considered'.

By way of example, here's a comparison of two jobs, User Experience Design and Digital Marketing Manager.

User Experience & Design	*Digital Marketing Manager*

Criteria	Score		Criteria	Score
High salary	7		High salary	8
Ability to work remotely	8		Ability to work remotely	3
Rapid advancement	3		Rapid advancement	7
A job that is creative	9		A job that is creative	6
Job security	8		Job security	7
Total Score	35		Total Score	31

In this example, a User Experience and Design job provided a somewhat better career option than Digital Marketing Manager 'all things considered'. With this output, your next step would be to more deeply explore each job on your short-list by conducting online research including position descriptions on job boards such as Glassdoor.com Indeed.com, and the following websites:

- One To Online https://www.onetonline.org/

- U.S. Bureau of Labor Statistics https://www.bls.gov/ooh/
- My Next Move https://www.mynextmove.org/

Of course, the best source of feedback would be via direct conversations with people who currently work in your field of interest. Ask people in your network of friends and family if they can refer you to anyone. Also, go to LinkedIn.com and find the 'People' tab on the main navigation tab. Here you can search specific job titles and find the names and specific people holding those positions. Send a request to 'connect' to at least 25 people. Some will accept your invitation which will enable you to follow up with a 'message' asking them to speak with you and provide their first-hand insights. with those who currently work in the field. I'd also suggest using LinkedIn search to find school alumni to connect with and request career guidance. With a little effort, you should be able to find a friendly and valuable career mentor.

PLAY # 3 EXECUTION

Landing Your First Marketing Job

Certain jobs require highly specialized skills that are only obtained with extensive training and several years of experience. Others require just a nominal amount of training and experience, often obtainable online for free or at a nominal cost. We'll address these opportunities in the chapters ahead.

Most careers outlined in Section V of the book include suggestions for 'Landing Your First Job'. It's important to know that even a little hands-on experience can help secure that first job. I took a non-paying summer internship at a small direct marketing ad agency. This allowed me to add 'direct response marketing' experience to my resume and was the primary reason I landed my first marketing job.

PLAY # 4: Long-Term Career Success

The saying 'change is the only constant' perfectly describes a marketing career. To advance your career you'll need to relentlessly develop your skills, managerial competencies, and your personal attributes. Too often I've seen very talented people rest on their laurels and not invest in their professional growth. They 'hit the glass ceiling' far too young, or worse, lose their job during all-too-common reorganizations.

The following provides my thoughts on some of the critical skills, competencies, and personal attributes needed by current and future marketing leaders.

Essential Marketing Skills
- Marketing strategy fundamentals – no matter how long one has worked in marketing, a 'refresher' in the foundations is always a good idea.
- Contemporary marketing research methodologies – this is essential given the rapid advancements in data and digital technology.
- Integrated digital marketing communication strategy – digital now 'rules the roost' and has significantly changed the rules of consumer engagement.
- Marketing technology fundamentals – 21st-century marketers must understand the technology that powers media, content, analytics, and CRM.
- Omni Channel Marketing – this field represents modern Customer Relationship Management.

- Marketing analytics – artificial intelligence is radically altering this field building on existing capabilities such as Advanced Segmentation, Descriptive Analytics, Predictive Modeling, Marketing Mix & Attribution Modeling.
- Data management fundamentals – with the explosion of AI, it's really important to understand 'the basics' of data collection, processing, and analysis.
- Customer Journey Mapping & User Experience – no marketing plan can be considered 'consumer-centric with these essential contemporary practices.

Essential Managerial Competencies

- Teamwork and collaboration – you can't succeed in business going it alone. '
- Clarity of communication – the ability to clearly and concisely write, speak, and present is a major career differentiator.
- A global perspective – the world will continue to become 'smaller' providing new opportunities to create business value and advance your career.
- Managing change and complexity – this is perhaps the toughest competency for any businessperson to tackle today.
- Resolving conflicts for win-win situations – an essential competency for sustained career growth (and survival).
- Empowering others – this means hiring good people and letting them do their job! (This lesson took many years for me to learn!).

Essential Personal Attributes

- Integrity and honesty – business is a 'one strike' game and you will never have a second chance to the trusted.
- Embracing diversity & inclusion – in addition to being a moral imperative, it's also good for business.

- Finding work-life balance – this is easier said than done!

Creating Your Career Curriculum

To remain 'on your game', take advantage of career development programs offered at your company. Too often opportunities to learn new skills, or refresh existing ones are not embraced because people are 'just too busy'. But in the long run, you are passing up an investment worth tens of thousands of dollars. Each year I would set a goal to attend at least two major company-sponsored career development events. This required me to work some nights and weekends to catch up on my job responsibilities, but it paid off in the long run.

If you want to truly remain 'relevant' as a marketer, you'll also need to develop your personal skill development curriculum. For me, this meant tackling those skills in which I was 'average' and continuously exploring consumer and marketing trends. I always envied my colleagues with superb presentation skills, and I was only 'so so'. With a lot of practice, I went from being a 'terrible' presenter to a 'passable' one, which certainly helped my career longevity.

As a digital marketer, it was obvious to me that having a deep understanding of data and technology was essential. Since I did not go through any deep schooling in these areas, I forced myself to advance my knowledge in these areas. I tutored myself by reading (boring) books, reading articles, attending conferences, and always asking questions to IT and analytics partners.

The following section lists some of the resources I've taken advantage of in my personal quest for career relevancy.

Free Training Courses

- Google Skill Shop offers several digital advertising courses and certifications https:// skillshop.withgoogle.com

- Salesforce Trailhead offers courses and certifications in many advanced and emerging areas https://trailhead.salesforce.com/
- HubSpot Academy offers many courses including content marketing, email marketing, search marketing, and web development https://academy.hubspot.com/
- SEMRush provides expert search engine optimization courses https://www.semrush.com/academy/courses/seo-toolkit-course/
- Meta offers a comprehensive program for social media marketing https://www.facebook.com/business/learn/social-media-marketing-certificate-coursera

Other free courses are offered by Coursera (https://www.coursera.org), Udemy (udemy.com), and Skillshare (skillshare.com).

Free Newsletters
- Deloitte Consulting https://www2.deloitte.com/lt/en/misc/subscribe-form.html
- Boston Consulting Group https://www.bcg.com/subscription/subscription
- McKinsey https://www.mckinsey.com/capabilities/growth-marketing-and-sales/newsletter-sign-up
- IBM https://www.ibm.com/subscribe/
- Harvard Business Review https://hbr.org/email-newsletters

Podcasts
Forbes Magazine has compiled this excellent list of the best marketing podcasts https://www.forbes.com/sites/henrydevries/2018/08/20/the-eight-best-marketing-podcasts/?sh=637d86b37b00

Books
- *Ogilvy on Advertising* by David Ogilvy
- *Permission Marketing* by Seth Godin

- *Positioning: The Battle for The Mind* by Jack Trout and Al Ries
- *The Global Brand CEO* by Mark de Swaan Arons and Frank van den Driest
- *Influence: The Psychology of Persuasion* by Robert Cialdini
- *The Innovator's Dilemma* by Clayton Christensen
- *Eating The Big Fish: How Challenger Brands Van Compete Against Brand Leaders* by Adam Morgan
- *Big Data* by Viktor Mayer-Schönberger and Kenneth Cukier
- *Marketing Management* by Phillip Kotler
- *Converge: Transforming Business at The Intersection of Marketing and Technology* by Bob Lord and Ray Velez

Conferences

- Gartner Marketing Symposium https://www.gartner.com/en/conferences
- Salesforce Dreamforce
- Adobe Summit https://summit.adobe.com/na/
- Inbound https://www.inbound.com/
- MarTech https://martech.org/conference/
- B2B Marketing Exchange https://b2bmarketing.exchange/
- Content Marketing World https://www.contentmarketingworld.com/
- Digital Summit https://digitalsummit.com/
- LeadsCon https://leadscon.com/event/leadscon-las-vegas-2022/

Career Development Planning Toolkit

You can only rely on yourself to advance your career – not your company or your boss. Developing, and regularly updating a written personal career curriculum is a 'smart way to stay smart'. Consider the following approach:

1. **Take A Career Development Assessment**

    a. What job would you like to have in 5-7 years from now? What are the skills and competencies required?

    b. How is your area of marketing expected to evolve? What new skills will likely be required in 5 years from now?

    c. Which existing skills do believe are subpar and that you need to improve?

    d. Which skills do you believe are 'good' but can become 'exceptional'?

2. **Define Your Development Goals**

    a. Which skills do you want to focus on over the next 12 months? Which do you want to focus on over the next 3 years?

    b. Which skills need to be 'expert' versus 'intermediate'?

    c. What combination of expert skills might accelerate your career?

    d. Which managerial competencies are essential for your 'perfect' job? Which needs the most maturing short term?

3. **Career Development Activities**

In addition to the education & training resources noted earlier, other development activities you can pursue include:

    a. Job-Based Activities – including job rotations, 'stretch assignments', cross-functional projects, task forces, teaching others, etc.

    b. Relationship-Based Activities – including mentoring, job-shadowing, networking, meeting with subject matter experts, etc.

'There is no finish line' when it comes to growing as a

professional.

V. DETAILED CAREER DESCRIPTIONS

This section organizes career options based on the four primary marketing activities: with Digital Marketing and Non-Digital Marketing careers discussed within each.

- **Market & Customer Insights** describes client-side (not ad agency) careers responsible for understanding the customer, the competition, and other external influences on the business. Customer understanding guides all elements of the marketing program and is the job's primary responsibility. Careers outlined include Marketing Research Management, User Experience Research Management, and other related careers.

- **Strategic Marketing** describes career options focused on planning and overseeing all, or most components of the marketing program. Careers outlined include Product Management, Brand Management, and E-Commerce Management, Corporate Brand Management, Digital Marketing Campaign Management, Integrated Marketing Communication Management, Demand Generation Management, and related Strategic Marketing careers.

- **Marketing Execution** explains those careers that bring to life the marketing strategy. These jobs mainly focus on planning and/or executing the 'Promotion' component of the '4Ps' of marketing. Careers outlined include Advertising Management, Digital Media Management, Search Engine Optimization (SEO) Management, Paid Search (SEM - Search Engine Marketing), Social Media Manager, Social Media Community Manager, Content Marketing Strategist, User Experience Management, User Interface Management, Consumer Promotion Management, Shopper Marketing, Trade Marketing, and

Marketing Automation Management.

- **Measurement & Optimization** describes careers focused on measuring and analyzing marketing program results including Marketing Analyst, Data Scientist, and related Measurement & Optimization.

The most common (or emerging) career opportunities within each section are then outlined as follows:

- Typical Job Descriptions
- Success Criteria – the skills and competencies crit ical for success in the job
- Pros and Cons - the good and bad things to consider about this career track
- Career Path – future career path opportunities
- Salary Guidance – salary range estimated per job
- Landing Your First Job – suggestions for breaking into the field

The essence of competitive advantage is having knowledge that others do not. Market & Customer Insights provides this knowledge and guides management's understanding of where the market is going, what customers need, how customers buy, what prices they are willing to pay, and how to generate customer demand for the product.

To quote a lyric from a Grateful Dead song— 'Once in a while, you get shown the light in the strangest of places if you look at it right'. UUnique customer insights are responsible for all great product innovations. Steve Jobs recognized that a computer could be an extension of the individual and a powerful tool for creative, intellectual, and personal expression—and not simply a 'business machine'. Starbucks knew that a cup of coffee was more than a 'hot beverage', and recognized it as a moment of personal or social relaxation. Red Bull saw how a beverage could define a lifestyle and created an entirely new category. But there are also misguided insights that yielded true marketplace disasters such as the New Coke debacle of the 1980s. Great (or terrible) Market Research Management is the indispensable 'rudder' that points the marketing ship in the right direction.

The Work

Market and Customer Insight can involve understanding the customer, developing new products, or guiding more effective ways to advertise, promote, and package the product. Market researchers use a variety of 'qualitative' and 'quantitative' techniques to guide their work.

Qualitative Research is the starting point for most customer research and captures insights from just a handful of people by interviewing and/or observing them. Qualitative research is used only as a 'starting point' to guide further (quantitative) research and is never used to draw final conclusions. Qualitative research methods include:

- Focus Groups: these are forums led by a Moderator who interviews customers (usually 6 -10 people) to gain first-hand 'qualitative' feedback on a particular topic. Today, focus groups are largely conducted virtually via Zoom or similar platforms.
- Ethnography: this technique involves first-hand observation of customer behavior The market researcher simply watches the customer from a distance performing their 'usual routine' associated with a product i.e. how the customer shops and buys, how they use the product etc.
- Social Media Listening: social media interactions provide a robust tool to gather unique customer insights. Market researchers observe what brand fans (and brand detractors) are saying about the brand, the terminology they use, what content they engage with, etc.

Quantitative research gathers data (opinions, preferences, etc.) among a very large number of customers (hundreds if not thousands of customers) via surveys. Similar to political polling, a large sample of customers enable the market researcher to more accurately predict the opinions or preference of customers in the entire market.

Syndicated research gathers information from external, often no-cost data sources compiled by the U.S. Government, industry associations, Wall Street reports, and company annual reports, among others. Market researchers use these sources to understand population (demographic) trends, societal beliefs and values, and industry (market forecasts, competition) trends. Syndicated research is an essential tool for the market researcher to know where the customer and market stand today and where they are going.

As you might expect, digital technology has revolutionized

this field. The volume and variety of digital and social data available have grown exponentially over the last ten years. Also, advancements in computing technology and artificial intelligence now enable market researchers to deeply analyze this unprecedented volume of data.

MARKET RESEARCH MANAGER

Similar Titles: Customer Insights Manager, Market Research Analyst

The Market Research Manager provides the Brand Manager or Product Manager with the answers to the most important marketing strategy questions:

· Who are our customers and what do they need?

· How can we develop products that provide greater value to them?

· How should the product be designed or formulated to meet customer requirements?

· Which advertising campaign idea will be most effective?

· Where is the market going, and how will it look 5 years from now?

· How do customers view our brand versus that of the competition?

· What is the best way to segment the market and which customer segments offer the

  greatest business opportunity?

To answer these questions, the Market Research Manager needs to determine how to design the research, execute the study, and analyze and report the results. This begins with developing the 'research brief', a single document outlining the research objectives, the profile of the consumer to be researched, the sample size, research timing, budget, etc. The Manager then decides which type of research best answers the question at hand i.e., should the research be qualitative (direct feedback from customers via focus groups or one-on-one interviews) or quantitative (via surveys)? They will then create the tools and materials (questionnaires, discussion guides, etc.) to field the research.

Market Research Managers typically hire specialized market research vendors to execute the research. These vendors will do the leg-work of finding qualified participants for the research, and lead its implementation via qualitative or quantitative studies/

As the saying goes, 'garbage in = garbage out'. A focus group of consumers that don't really match the profile of the target audience or a poorly designed questionnaire is not only a waste of time and money but could also point the brand in the completely wrong direction. So ensuring pristine execution of the research is a major responsibility of the Market Research Manager.

Ttypical Job description

- Determine appropriate research activities to deliver unique and relevant customer and market insights.
- Meet with internal clients (Brand or Product Managers) to identify knowledge gaps and prioritize key business issues requiring market research.
- Assess and select the most appropriate methodologies and techniques to achieve the research objectives.
- Design quantitative research questionnaires and qualitative focus group moderation guides.
- Ensure third-party market research vendors deliver accurate, timely, and meaningful insights.
- Lead research to inform brand positioning, campaign development, and media.
- Analyze and interpret research data.
- Write research conclusions and present actionable recommendations to management.
- Use industry best practices to monitor industry, category, and competitive market dynamics.

A Typical WorkWeek

· Present the latest competitive activity data to the marketing department

· Present brand positioning research conclusions to the advertising agency

· Working lunch with this evening's focus group moderator
· Review vendor proposals for testing copy for the new ad campaign
· Present social media 'listening' report to the Brand Manager
· Review esults of the new website user experience study
· Prepare for tomorrow's presentation on market trends to the Division President
· Prepare the moderation guide for next week's online consumer focus group

Career Path & Salaries* (*Salaries based on mid-large companies)

- Entry-Level: Market Research Analyst: $45k - $85k
- Mid-Level: Market Research Manager: $90k - $130k (+ 15–20% annual bonus)
- Senior-Level: Market Research Director: $100k - $180k (+ 20–30% bonus)

Job Outlook

The market research job outlook is very promising. The U.S. Bureau of Labor Statistics projects that 165,000 new market research jobs will be created between 2020 and 2030.

Success Factors
Skills

· Superior knowledge of market research models and methodologies including qualitative, quantitative, ad-hoc, and syndicated research
· Strong project management skills
· Superior analytical abilities including advanced statistics
· Superior written and oral communication skills

Competencies

· Strong interpersonal skills and the ability to work collaboratively
· Strong influencing skills

· bility to multi-task and manage multiple priorities
· Strong ability to work effectively under tight timelines
· Superior passion for understanding consumer needs,
habits, attitudes, and opinions

Pros/Cons

Pros

- You can make a major impact on serving the needs of customers and the success of the business
- It's a highly strategic role
- It can be less stressful than other marketing jobs
- Decent work-life balance (most of the time)
- You work with smart people within a variety of marketing roles
- Excellent future job prospects
- Good pay

Cons

- It's a somewhat 'behind-the-scenes' role
- Much narrower in scope than Brand or Product Manager roles

Landing Your First Job

Breaking into market research, as with most marketing jobs, requires some 'proof points', and securing an internship in market research or data analytics would be the best place to start. Contact focus groups and/or quantitative research companies in your area. They often need well-spoken and organized people to find consumers to participate in research and to help coordinate the fielding of their quantitative and qualitative research programs.

Look on the websites of such companies such as Verizon, Gartner, Field Nation, Boston Strategy, and VDC Research offer market research internship. However, any internship that involves analytical work can also provide some level of experience.

You could also volunteer to conduct research for a local business and offer to:
- assess their Facebook or Twitter conversations
- analyze their sales data for insights into the business

- analyze the behavior of their customers within their store
You would then write your conclusions and present them to the local business owner. You've then created your first 'proof point' which should impress many potential future employers.

You can also use LinkedIn to contact market research managers and seek their guidance for breaking into the field.

The Bottom Line
Market Research Management is a great career choice for the right individual. You'll work with smart people, be at the forefront of your industry, and have an opportunity to make a significant impact. As discussed in the Marketing Strategy section, you won't be 'the lead actor' in the play, but rather a critical supporting actor. This role is just fine with many talented people while others may find it too specialized.

User Experience (UX) Researcher
We all have experienced websites that just 'work right'—those sites that seem to sense what we are looking for and how we look for it. With just two or three clicks we effortlessly land on a webpage with the information we were seeking. Of course, we have all also experienced websites that are confusing and frustrating to navigate. Achieving the former and preventing the latter is the role of the User Experience Researcher.

The User Experience Researcher is responsible for designing and conducting research to optimize the navigation, design, layout, and functionality of web and mobile digital properties. The ultimate goal is to ensure that visitors find the information they are looking for in an easy, fast, and 'intuitive' manner.

The best User Experience Research Managers combine expert knowledge of digital technology with a deep understanding of how people use digital media. 'Usability research' is the primary tool used and places actual consumers in front of a website (or a website prototype). The UX manager directs them through a series of 'tasks' and observes the actions of consumers as they try to achieve them. Was it difficult to navigate the site? Could they find the desired information once they navigated to the correct page, and did this information enable them to complete the given task?

The UX Manager also explores how consumers interact with site applications and other functionality e.g., was the shopping cart easy to use? Was it placed on the correct webpage? Was it located in the right area of the page? With this information, the User Experience Manager will brief all parties (marketer, information architect, UX designer, etc.) on areas requiring further optimization.

This is a highly skilled profession requiring training and hands-on experience. However, employer demand for these valuable skills is great and will continue to increase in the years ahead.

Overview

UX research seeks to understand the motivations, needs, and goals of the customer when engaging with a digital product. A 'user experience journey map' is the primary output of the research. This tool maps the sequential steps taken by customers when researching or buying a product online. The user experience researcher studies each step of the journey to understand the primary purpose of the brand's website within the customer's digital journey. Having this information informs the user experience researcher about how to optimize the site's design, navigation, interactivity, and content.

Typical Job description

- Understand and document customers' digital product research needs, challenges, and problems.
- Uncover customer insights that lead to more compelling and user-friendly digital experiences.
- Apply user experience design research principles including face-to-face interviews, user surveys and questionnaires, card sorting, concept testing, user groups, and usability testing.
- Ddevelop 'journey maps' to uncover moments of user frustrations when experiencing the digital product.
- Test different versions of the digital experiences via the website and mobile app prototypes.
- Create a holistic view of how customers experience the digital product.
- Write and present clear and insightful reports to management.

A Typical WorkWeek

A typical work week of the User Experience Manager can vary significantly depending on the stage of the research project. Some weeks will involve extensive preparation for user research groups, while others will involve working side by side with users (customers) to capture and document their feedback. The latter stages of the project will focus on summarizing and reporting the conclusions and recommendations of the research.

Career Path & Salaries* (*Salaries based on mid-large companies)

Entry-level salaries are in the $70k - $80k range. More experienced user experience research managers earn on average $100k although the range can be between $85k and $120k.

Job Outlook

User experience research managers are in high demand with outstanding future job growth very likely.

Success Factors

Skills

· Experience with advanced UX research methods e.g., journey maps, usability testing, card sorting, and heuristic evaluation.
· Understanding of user-centered and interaction design principles.

· Ability to 'conceptualize' future product enhancements and innovations.
· Strong project management skills.
· Superior written and oral communication skills.

Competencies

· Strong interpersonal skills and the ability to work collaboratively with cross-functional teams.
· Relentless 'curiosity' for understanding how consumers use technology
· Strong ability to multi-task and manage multiple priorities.
· Strong ability to work effectively under tight timelines.

Pros/Cons

Pros

- Leading-edge digital career path
- You will play a key role in defining next-generation digital products
- Decent work-life balance (most of the time)
- You work with highly creative and tech-savvy people
- Excellent current and future job prospects
- High pay

Cons

- The available budget sometimes limits the ability to deliver a great user experience
- Everyone in the organization will have an opinion and you will frequently need to 'defend' your work

Landing Your First Job

Breaking into user experience research will require hands-on training. Explore university programs (e.g. Michigan, UCLA) that offer online courses and certifications. Also, read this excellent article by someone who has done it: **'How I Broke Into UX Research Without Any Experience'**: https://uxplanet.org/how-i-broke-into-ux-research-with-no-prior-experience-7bf137e2ba31

The Bottom Line

User Experience Research is a fascinating and growing profession. You will learn highly valuable and unique skills that will always be in demand by employers. You will be an 'explorer' of customer needs and an 'architect' who designs digital solutions to meet these. You'll work with creative and tech-savvy people, and have the ability to leave your mark on the future of digital technology.

Market research managers rely on external vendors to perform several specialized research activities. Brief explanations of these are provided below.

Qualitative Research Analyst

The Qualitative Research Analyst works face-to-face with consumers to gain a deep understanding of the question at hand—their shopping habits, perceptions of the brand or competitors, what they think of a new product idea, etc. They will design and field the research through various methods such as focus groups, one-on-one interviews, and ethnographic research (live observations of consumers in their homes or the store shopping).

Quantitative Research Analyst

Before investing millions of dollars into a new product or advertising campaign, marketers can't simply rely on qualitative research. Quantitative research is used to test marketing ideas with large and 'statistically significant' samples of consumers to provide marketers with much greater confidence in their decisions.

The Quantitative Research Analyst designs and implements this research via online, telephone, mail, and in-person surveys. They develop the sampling plan (who and how many should we research?) and prepare the questionnaire and other material needed for the research. The Analyst will then organize all fieldwork re

quired to distribute and collect the surveys, interpret the results, and present their written findings to the client.

This role requires strong quantitative and statistical skills, and an ability to interpret data and translate it into actionable feedback.

Syndicated Research Management

Companies rely on many forms of information to guide their business decisions e.g. economic data, consumer trends, demographic (population) data, etc. These are typically very extensive and complex reports, and far too expensive for any company to pay for on their own.

Syndicated research managers lead the collection and analysis of insights from information available publicly via published reports and open databases The syndicated research manager works with managers within their company to define their market intelligence needs and then scours external data sources to address them. This role requires deep research and analytical skills, and the ability to clearly articulate findings through written reports and in-person presentations.

Focus Group Moderator

Focus groups are frequently used as the starting point for capturing customer insights. The group consists of a small number of people (usually 8 – 10 strangers) who are led by the moderator in an in-depth discussion on a particular topic. Topics vary significantly but usually explore how people purchase and use a product, and/or how they perceive a particular brand. It's the job of the

focus group moderator to encourage a group of strangers to 'open up' and speak their minds on the topic at hand.

Focus groups provide marketers with 'directional' feedback from consumers. Thus, the research findings are useful, but inconclusive, and not used to make final marketing decisions. The focus group moderator plans and leads ('facilitates'), working from a structured set of questions that they have designed.

A 'great' focus group happens when all participants are 'leaning in' and openly sharing their honest thoughts. A 'bad' focus group happens when one person monopolizes the entire conversation and makes it difficult for anyone else to contribute. An important job of the focus group moderator is to prevent this and ensure that everyone contributes to the discussion. Once the focus group has concluded, the moderator then writes a report to 'crystallize' the collective opinions of the group about the topic at hand and provide these conclusions and recommendations to the client.

All marketing roles require some degree of 'strategy'. However, this section will outline a handful of career paths that are responsible for leading strategic areas that are core to the overall business:

- Product Management / Digital Product Management
- Brand Management
- E-Commerce Management
- Corporate Brand Strategy
- Digital Marketing (Campaign) Management
- Integrated Marketing Communication Management

Product and Brand Management

There are some nuances between Product and Brand Management which are outlined in this section. However, both roles are fundamentally about growing the business and running the business. This includes developing the marketing strategy and business plan for a product (or a group of products) or service and directing the execution of the '4 Ps of Marketing'—the Product to sell, the Price to sell it at, the Place(s) to distribute it and how to Promote it via the marketing communication mix. Product and Brand Management roles are true 'mini CEOs' within their companies.

It All Began with Procter and Gamble

The concept of 'Brand Management' was a revolutionary concept when first introduced by Procter & Gamble in the 1930s. P&G competed in many product categories and sold several different brands within each. The goal of the brand management model was to ensure that their respective brands did not compete with one another. This required that each brand be 'differentiated' by distinctly catering to different types of consumer needs. Over the years, P&G mastered the art & science of Brand Management including such fundamental principles as the 'unique selling proposition', 'brand positioning,' and 'branding'. The company also pioneered the field of consumer research and the use of mass media (TV and Radio) to promote brands.

Modern-day 'Brand' and 'Product' Management within any company is derived from the P&G model. But what's the same and what's different?

What's The Same?
Both Brand and Product Management roles are responsible for having a deep understanding of the customer and the marketplace. Both are 'mini-CEO' roles that have overall responsibility for the success of a specific product or brand. Product and brand managers develop the overall business plan and have ownership of the P&L (profit & loss) statement. Both roles lead the development of the marketing strategy and determine how to segment the market, select the target audience, and define how to differentiate and position the product. Lastly, both brand

and product managers have responsibility for creating and executing the marketing program that will create customer demand for the product.

What's Different?
'Brand' versus 'Product' management titles differ largely based on the type of industry. The Brand Manager title is primarily used in a company that sells the 'consumer packaged goods' (CPG) found on grocery store shelves, drug stores, and other mass merchandisers. Brand managers have responsibility for all elements of the brand marketing plan. They lead new

product development, and determine the product's price, and where it will be sold. Central to this role is crafting how the brand will be 'positioned' to the customer. Effective positioning distinguishes the brand from competitive brands, and via marketing communication, answers the question 'why should the customer buy my brand versus any other'?

The product manager title is most commonly used at non-CPG companies with more complex products e.g. information technology, telecommunications, medical equipment etc. Unlike brand managers, product managers have limited influence over product development and innovation since these decisions are usually led by Engineering and/or R&D. The majority of their time is spent leading the other aspects of the marketing mix: price, distribution, and promotion. Product managers also are responsible for defining the product's positioning strategy and communicating this to customers via

marketing communication channels e.g. TV advertising, social media, the brand website, e-mail marketing, etc.

Brand Management

As noted, the term Brand Management is typically found within CPG (Consumer Packaged Goods) companies. The core responsibility of the brand manager is to grow the revenue, market share, and profitability of the brand. Thus, brand managers have the great responsibility of 'owning' the P&L (Profit and Loss Statement) and are in the 'hot seat' to deliver financial results.

Brand managers develop the overall business plan, the heart of which is the marketing strategy. Thus, the brand manager has responsibility for product development, as well as the pricing, distribution, and promotion (including advertising) strategies.

The marketing strategy is a comprehensive plan that addresses key questions such as:
- What is the brand strategy and positioning to distinguish it in the market?
- What new products will be introduced? When? At what price?
- What ad campaign(s) will be developed? How much should be spent on media?
- How much will be invested in consumer promotions?
- What new distribution channels should be considered?
- What special pricing and deals should be implemented on the store shelf?

Once the plan is completed, the brand manager must 'sell' his or her plan to senior management. These meetings can be brutally tough and require convincing the 'powers that be' (including the finance director) to approve the requested marketing program funding.

With the plan approved, the brand manager 'runs the business', and leads a large team of professionals inside and outside the company to execute the plan. These include:
- the advertising agency
- consumer promotion
- trade promotion
- finance
- market research
- research & development
- packaging design
- media
- legal

Brand management provides unmatched business training and is the pathway to senior management at CPG companies. So, if running a large business—with someone else's money—at a very young age sounds interesting, consider the Brand Management career path.

Job Responsibilities

- Lead the development of the business plan for the brand, establishing sales, market share, and profit objectives.
- Develop a marketing strategy that delivers sales, profit, and market share targets.
- Develop compelling and differentiating brand strategy and positioning.
- Lead the planning of all marketing communication including advertising, digital and social media.
- Lead promotion planning including the alignment of trade, shopper, and consumer promotions.
- Develop the pricing strategy that maximizes sales and gross profit.
- Lead new product development.
- Guide market research to understand market trends, and customer needs and motivations.
- Measure and report marketing campaign performance metrics.

Typical Work Week

· Meet with sales and operations directors to update the sales forecast

· Lead product innovation planning meeting with Research & Development

· Meet with ad agency to review TV ad storyboards and media plan

· Review new website design and social media program results

· Prepare for the monthly meeting to present business results to the division president

· Meet with market research manager to review the new market research brief

· Prepare a presentation to showcase the new product launch at

the national sales
  meeting.

Career Path and Salaries

Your first job will be as an assistant brand manager (brand assistant) for a specific brand, working directly for the brand manager. Training programs vary significantly across companies, but you will likely be given responsibility for a set of specialized tasks such as managing the sales forecast, analyzing market data, or running a social media marketing program. A good training program will expose you to all critical aspects of running the business, essentially trailing your brand manager to key strategic, advertising, sales, and other meetings.

Your first promotion (within 1 - 2 years) is to associate brand manager, where you will get meatier responsibilities—perhaps leading the national consumer or trade promotion programs. Once you have proven proficiency across the '4Ps', you'll earn your brand manager stripe (usually within 3 - 5 years). The next rung on the ladder is marketing director (7 – 10 years). This level is also referred to as group marketing manager or category manager and is responsible for a portfolio of brands within a specific category (e.g., Nestle's coffee brands). Vice president of marketing comes next (10 - 15+ years) and has responsibility for all brands within a specific line of business (e.g., all beverage or all snack brands within the company).

Brand management is the path to the top of the ladder, CEO, within a CPG company. Unlike other functions such as finance and sales, the marketer will already have a deep understanding of the consumer, the marketplace, and how to grow a profitable business.

Salaries vary widely depending on if you have an MBA if you are with a large CPG company, and if you live in a major metro area. The following is a rough estimate of compensation in companies with $1 billion or more in sales revenue:

Assistant Brand Manager $75k - $100k plus a 10 - 15% bonus
Brand Manager $90k - $120k plus a 15 - 20% bonus
Marketing Director $140k - $200k plus a 20 - 30% bonus
Marketing VP $200k - $350k plus a 30 - 50% bonus

Job Outlook

The Bureau of Labor Statistics expects advertising, promotion, and marketing management jobs to grow by 10% between 2020 and 2030. That's only 1% growth per year but still equates to over 30,000 new jobs.

Pros/Cons

Pros

- Exceptional business training
- Highly entrepreneurial role
- Lots of responsibility at a young age
- The ability to run your own business
- No two days are the same
- The fastest route to executive management
- Combines 'business' acumen with 'creative' ability
- You work with a variety of people and professions
- Very good compensation
- Rapid career advancement

Cons

- You typically manage 'not-so-sexy' consumer brands
- Often very stressful
- Not a 9-to-5 job. Expect long hours
- Intense competition for promotions
- Executive jobs are ultra-competitive

Success Factors

Successful brand managers have a combination of entrepreneurial, strategic thinking, leadership, and planning capabilities. It's truly a multi-dimensional role that wears many hats and interacts with everyone in the organization. The brand manager must be able to 'talk shop' with the deep-thinking scientists in R&D, gain the trust and partnership of the hard-charging sales force, and guide the work of the ad agency and promotion department. The best brand managers work hard to earn the respect of all functions within the business.

Skills Required

- Strong business judgment and the ability to see the 'big picture'
- Strong quantitative aptitude
- Strong written and verbal communication skills
- Superior project management skills
- Deep understanding of traditional, digital, and social media communication channels

Competencies Required

- Superior leadership skills
- Superior interpersonal skills
- Solid creative thinking abilities
- Superior 'self-starter' requiring limited supervision
- Strong entrepreneurial drive

Landing Your First Job

An entry-level brand management job at a large company usually requires an MBA, and typically from a top school. However, a BS/MS degree in marketing is sometimes acceptable if the candidate has solid work experience in a related area such as advertising, promotion, or sales.

Even with an MBA, many companies still expect some marketing-related prior experience—whether it be at a small company or a summer internship. When interviewing, it is critical to highlight your entrepreneurial experiences and ambitions. Even if you haven't started your own business, bring a well-thought-through 'voice of the customer' perspective. Go buy the company's products, spend some time using them, and consider how the marketing program might be improved. Recommending enhancements to their advertising, digital strategy, or packaging design will enable you to stand out during the interview process. It doesn't matter if your recommendations are right or wrong. You just want to show that

you're a 'thinker'. There are many 'doers' but only a few who can create the future.

The Bottom Line

A Brand Management career will not only provide you with unmatched training in marketing but also develop your general management and entrepreneurial abilities. You will be running 'a company within a company' with full P&L responsibility.

You'll be the king or queen of the castle and the master of your domain. The pressure will be on you to 'deliver' your business plan, or you will be 'dethroned'. You will work with a variety of functions within the organization including sales, finance, operations, and information technology and no day is ever 'routine'. Brand management provides you with a lot of responsibility at an early age, and places you on the 'executive track' with the potential to rise to senior management jobs including the Chief Executive Officer.

Product Manager

Product managers are responsible for a single product line (e.g., home printers), and lead marketing planning and execution for a new and/or existing product. They work closely with sales to expand the distribution of the product into various distribution channels and establish pricing. They also lead the development of marketing communication and promotion programs including

trade shows, trade promotion, advertising, consumer promotion, and digital marketing programs.

In B2C companies, product managers drive customer demand using the same type of advertising and promotional programs we reviewed in the Brand Management section. In B2B companies, they are tasked with developing 'demand generation' marketing programs that channel new customer 'leads' to the sales force. Demand generation uses advertising, digital, and social media programs to capture the attention of potential customers and encourage them to provide their contact information (name, e-mail address, phone number). This contact information is then given to the sales force to follow up and close the sale.

Job Responsibilities
- Lead the product marketing process including market and customer insights, strategic planning, marketing execution, and measurement.
- Plan and execute marketing programs to generate and nurture sales leads.
- Lead the new product launch planning process across key functional teams including R&D, Engineering, and Marketing Communications.
- Lead planning for all marketing communication including advertising, digital, and social media.
- Plan and implement loyalty-building Customer Relationship Marketing programs.
- Maintain a leading-edge understanding of industry trends and customer needs.
- Develop the pricing strategy that maximizes sales

velocity as well as gross profit.
- Prepare marketing materials to support the sales force and key customer accounts.
- Measure and report marketing campaign performance metrics.

A Typical WorkWeek
· Prep for a new product trade show with the event team
· Meet with a key customer about a new co-marketing program
· Review the new price elasticity study
· Update the holiday sales forecast with the sales director
· Release the new dealer incentive program to the sales force
· Meet with the digital marketing team to review search, website, and social results
· Meet with the ad agency to update them on the new promotional program
· Attend a department meeting to review & discuss new competitive activity

Career Path & Salaries (Mid to large sized companies)
The career path of a Product Manager varies significantly from company to company. But most companies follow the Assistant to Manager to Director to Vice President ladder. As you rise in the ranks, you will gain responsibility for an increasingly larger portfolio of products. When you achieve the role of Director (5 - 7 years) you will usually have responsibility for managing a portfolio of products. Here you will need to make decisions about

which market segments to target and develop the marketing program to drive customer demand within each segment.

At the vice president of marketing level (10 - 15+ years), you will manage all products within your division. In this role, you will also work with the product development team to determine the company's next-generation innovations and/or new acquisitions.

Product management is indeed a route to senior management, but unlike in a CPG company, not necessarily to the CEO job. Depending on the industry or company, management in other functions such as Sales, Engineering, or Finance may be considered better candidates for running the company.

Product management salaries vary widely. The following provides a rough guide to salaries at companies with $1B + revenue:
· Product Manager $100k - $160k plus a 15 - 20% bonus
· Marketing Director $140k - $180k plus a 20 - 30% bonus
· Marketing VP $180k - $280k plus a 30 - 50% bonus

Job Outlook
Job prospects for product management are strong. In fact, product management ranks fifth on Glassdoor's list of best jobs in America, with over 11,000 job opportunities available.

Success Factors
Great Product Managers know their market and customers better than anyone on the planet. They are leaders

who motivate and mobilize sales, advertising, promotion, and others within the organization. Success is based on the depth of their strategy, their ability to effectively execute marketing programs, and to quickly course-correct their program as market dynamics rapidly change.

Skills Required
· Superior business judgment
· Strong strategic planning aptitude
· Strong quantitative aptitude
· Solid writing and verbal communication skills
· Strong organizational skills

Competencies Required
· Strong leadership skills
· Superior interpersonal skills, especially with the salesforce
· Solid creative thinking abilities
· Superior 'self-starter' requiring limited supervision
· Strong 'team player'

Pros/Cons
Pros

- You usually work in dynamic industries such as technology and healthcare
- You get lots of responsibility quickly
- No two days are the same
- There is good career advancement potential
- You can make a real difference in the success of your company
- You work with a variety of people and professions
- The pay is generally very good

Cons

- You have limited responsibilities for new product development (although this is changing at some companies)
- The jobs can be highly stressful
- There are often long hours and frequent travel
- There is intense competition for promotions
- Rising to the executive ranks is ultra-competitive

Landing Your First Job
Entry-level product management jobs are possible, but almost always require an MBA and some prior work (or internship) experience. However product managers most frequently are sourced from personnel in the sales or marketing communication departments.

If you have a passion for a particular industry, assess any entry-level options. Consider first joining the company in a sales role. Sales experience provides excellent industry training, and if you can demonstrate strong strategic and business management skills, you should be a prime candidate for a Product Manager role within 2-3 years.

While product management might be a challenging field to land one's first job, more and more companies are addressing the need for strategic 'customer and market' oriented talent. They also desperately need digitally savvy people to bring their marketing programs into the 21st century. So there is a lot of opportunity once you get your foot in the door.

The Bottom Line

A product management career provides exceptional training in marketing while building strong general management capabilities. You will play point for all key decisions about your product and essentially be running 'a company within a company'. You will have an important job that impacts and interacts with many people in the organization.

There are no 'routine' days, and you will 'play point' and coordinate activities across sales, research and development, engineering, finance, customer service, and marketing communications. You will also be making decisions about where to spend millions of dollars. This is a terrific career path for those who want to develop their full capabilities as a marketer and general manager.

RELATED CAREERS

Digital Product Manager

Digital product manager roles lead innovation across specialized technology products such as software, tech hardware, websites, streaming services, cloud services, and mobile and social media apps.

Job Responsibilities

Digital Product Managers lead the product development strategy, define the product's features, and create the roadmap for marketing launch. This requires the ability to work in cross-functional teams that include people from user experience design, engineering, and marketing.

This role is not responsible for managing all of the '4 Ps' of marketing or running the end-to-end business. Rather, digital product managers are laser-focused on product innovation and how to optimize the 'user experience' of the product. Thus, the role is deeply involved in capturing customer insights to guide their development work.

Skills/Competencies

These roles are both strategic and tactical, 'playing point' across engineering, sales, marketing, and operations. Success thus requires strong project management, leadership, and collaboration skills.

Job Outlook

The job outlook for this career path is outstanding. Although no data exists for 'digital', product management is one of the top fields for anticipated job growth in the years ahead.

Landing Your First Job

Given how specialized this role is, I would strongly suggest that you reach out to people (on LinkedIn, college alumni, etc.) who are currently digital product managers and get their feedback on the education and training required to enter the field. Becoming certified in key principles such as User Center Design, UX and UI Design could each provide a valuable foundation.

E-commerce Marketing Management

Global e-commerce sales are currently about $1.5 trillion and rising at a double-digit rate. Almost all retail growth occurring was driven by internet versus physical store sales. e-commerce has had a significant impact on many industries. Media was the first to feel the impact as the convenience and value of online buying resulted in the shuttering of most book, music, and video retailers. 'Showrooming'—or the practice of checking out a product in the physical store, and then buying it for the lowest possible price online, has presented many challenges for retailers in all industries, especially electronics.

But even now, industries that seemed relatively sheltered from the e-commerce onslaught, such as furniture and clothing, are getting very (very) nervous. There is no re

versing this course—the only question is when will 'e-commerce' simply be referred to as 'commerce'.

Job Responsibilities

The E-commerce Marketing Manager leads strategic planning and execution for a brand's or retailer's online store. This is an extremely competitive space, and the e-Commerce Manager plays a critical role in the success or failure of the business.

The e-commerce manager develops the online retail strategy, determining what should be sold, how it is merchandised, and how it is priced. They then develop a promotional plan to 'find' prospective buyers through digital advertising, search, and social media to motivate them to visit their website. The e-commerce manager then plans the pricing, promotions, and product assortment tactics to motivate shoppers to select a product, place it in the e-shopping cart, and complete the purchase.

The great thing about e-commerce is that everything is measurable—every dollar spent can be evaluated against sales generated. The e-commerce manager relentlessly collects and analyzes data to update and optimize their programs—literally on a daily or even hourly basis. It's an intense role but one with a clear end game – maximizing sales and profitability.

e-Commerce management responsibilities vary significantly by type of industry. A media company (such as

Disney) will define the role differently than a cosmetics company. Also, a pure-play e-retailer (e.g., Amazon) will have somewhat different job requirements than a retailer selling both online and in physical stores (e.g., Walmart). However, the core tenets of the job, strategy, execution, measurement, and optimization always hold true and form the basis of the following job description.

Typical Job Description
- Lead strategic planning for the e-commerce program to achieve defined revenue and profitability goals.
- Create the online merchandising plan determining the optimal product assortment, placement, pricing, and promotional activity.
- Develop customer acquisition, conversion, and retention

campaigns. Lead the execution of paid search, SEO, digital advertising, web content, and landing pages, as well as social media, and e-mail marketing.

- Plan the e-commerce campaign calendar for key seasonal and promotional events.
- Implement A/B and multivariate testing programs to continually optimize program performance.
- Be a 'thought leader' in digital trends and online shopping behavior.

Typical Work Week
· Review campaign impact on sales with the analytics team and adjust advertising and

  promotion
· Meet with the merchandising team to update the product assortment mix
· Prepare the quarterly sales results for presentation to senior management
· Meet with Google and Facebook to review new targeted advertising programs
· Meet with the ad agency to review the new digital advertising campaign
· Meet with the IT department to demo the new shopping cart functionality
· Plan a multivariate test program for a new product line with the analytics team
· Scan competitive websites to assess their new merchandising programs

Career Path and Salaries
e-Commerce marketing manager salaries vary widely based on the size of the company, and the importance of online sales to the business. Salaries can range from as low as $50k, to as high as $125k, usually with 10 - 30% bonus potential.
e-Commerce IS the future of retailing and provides terrific

long-term career opportunities. Depending on the size of the company, your career path could lead from manager to director to VP of e-commerce and ultimately to CEO. But keep in mind that the competition in retailing, and especially online retailing, is brutal.

If the relentless pace of e-retailing becomes too much, you can easily make the transition to such roles as digi

tal marketing manager. Of course, if your ambition is to be an entrepreneur, you will also be well prepared to run your own e-commerce business!

Pros/Cons

Pros

- The multi-faceted digital marketing role
- The job is both strategic and creative
- You see the results of your work every day
- Strong future employment potential
- The pay can be very good
- Strong career potential
- Limited travel

Cons

- A very competitive, and thus very stressful field
- Your work is NEVER done....
- Can require very long hours
- Employment security can sometimes be unpredictable

Success Factors

The successful e-commerce manager is a digital marketing expert, as well as a retailer, entrepreneur, and shopper psychologist. The e-commerce manager must be 'fluent' in all things digital. In addition to having an expert grasp of the 'basics' (search marketing, web communication, digital advertising), they must also quickly embrace new digital technologies to improve the shopping experience and sales conversion.

The e-commerce manager is primarily a 'retailer' operating in a digital marketplace. Deep knowledge of current and future industry trends is essential to inform the most appropriate product assortment. The role requires an in-depth knowledge of online shopping behavior, and how pricing, promotions, and web content impact sales. A relentless thirst for finding unique shopper insights separates the 'good' from the 'outstanding' e-commerce manager.

Skills Required
- Superior knowledge of digital marketing channels and technology
- Strong strategic planning aptitude
- Strong quantitative aptitude
- Solid writing skills
- Solid verbal communication skills
- Strong organizational skills

Competencies Required
- Strong leadership skills
- Superior 'self-starter' requiring limited supervision
- Strong 'team player'
- Solid influencing skills
- Strong ability to multi-task and manage multiple priorities

Landing Your First Job
e-Commerce is all about retailing, just in a digital environment. Thus, any retailing job (in a store or online) is a good first step. Your ability to demonstrate that you can

'think like a shopper', understand their needs, and what

'triggers' a sale should impress any potential employer.

Take note of the difference between 'pure play' e-commerce companies such as amazon.com (which only sell online and do not have physical stores) versus hybrid retailers like Walmart (that sell both online and offline). Consider if your career ambitions are strictly 'online', or if you would prefer to work in both online and offline 'omni channel' retail environments.

Land your first job by first scouring job boards for entry-level or internship opportunities. Another way to get your foot in the door, is to reach out to a manager or executive at a company whose brands you know well. You would impress them by providing your analysis of their online shopping experience, and how you believe it could be improved. Start your analysis by having a specific 'shopping goal' i.e. 'I want to buy a new pair of earbuds that have great sounds and that perfectly fit my ears'. Then, begin your search for the earbuds and write down your answers these questions:

-   Where did you begin your online search online for the product? Search engine, social media, at a retail store?
-   Did you conduct a Google search, if so, did you see the brand listed on page one of the search engine rankings?
-   What were your first impressions when you landed on the brand's website?
-   Were the products presented in an 'enticing' way?

-   What ways did the site try to 'convert' you to an immediate sale?
-   How was the checkout process versus other e-retailers? etc.

No online retailer in the world delivers a 'perfect' shopping experience. Use your 'shopper-mindset' to demonstrate to a potential employer that you have an aptitude for such thinking. This capability should be held in high regard by a progressive company.

The Bottom Line

e-Commerce management includes some but not all of the responsibilities of Product and Brand Management. While this function is not responsible for product innovation, it is fully responsible for leading the online retailing strategy for a portfolio of products. This role leads many key activities including creating the online shopping 'experience', and the pricing, merchandising, and promotion mix.

e-commerce Merchandising Manager

Within large online retailers, there is frequently an e-commerce merchandising role dedicated to perfecting the merchandising mix. Key responsibilities include determining the product assortment, and how photos, videos, and other content are displayed on the website.

The e-Commerce merchandising manager needs a 'strategic' and 'creative' mind, strong analytical skills, as well as a keen eye for web design. Key responsibilities include planning the weekly and seasonal promotional offers, and leading the development of the web page content. To continually optimize program performance, the role requires extensive collaboration with the e-commerce manager, as well as the advertising, search marketing, and analytics teams.

Corporate Brand Management

A 'brand' is technically defined as the features (name, symbols, designs, etc.) that identify and distinguish one seller of a good or service from another. But this definition does not fully capture the importance (and financial value) of a brand as a company 'asset'. Someone much smarter than I said, 'products are produced in factories but brands are created in the mind'. Corporate brand management is the art and science of shaping how a brand is perceived by consumers, and why they should buy it versus competitive brands.

According to a 2020 Forbes measure, the Apple brand name is worth over $240 billion. Keep in mind that this figure does not include any of the 'tangible' assets (manufacturing plants, offices, inventory, cash, accounts receivable, etc.). This enormous amount is solely based on the 'intangible' value of Apple's brand equity.

This brand equity is driven by customers' experience with and/ or perceptions of the brand. Well-respected brands are more profitable because they have loyal customers eager to 'pull' the products off the shelf without price discounts. Premium brands also don't need to spend heavily on advertising and promotion. Less respected 'me too' brands have the opposite problem with the resulting negative impact on their bottom line.

The heart of brand management is the 'brand positioning statement', a strategic document that distinctly positions the brand in the mind of the customer. The goal is to find that 'position' that clearly defines what the brand stands for, what value it provides, and why it should be 'chosen' versus competitive offerings. Once established, the positioning statement serves as the guiding light for marketing communication activities including advertising, packaging, and promotional material.

Typical Job Description
- Develop the Corporate Brand Strategy including the brand positioning, marketing communication program, and measurement plan.
- Direct the Corporate Research team to develop brand insights utilizing syndicated research, qualitative research, and competitive assessments.
- Develop a compelling and distinctive brand positioning that strongly positions the brand in the mind of customers.
- Guide the planning and execution of external marketing communication by the ad agency, advertising, and digital marketing teams.
- Define brand development measurement goals and metrics. Work with market research to implement the measurement research.

- Review the creative team's updated brand logo recommendations.
- Work closely with company divisions, regions, and internal functions (such as HR, Investor Relations, etc.) to shape brand perceptions among business partners, prospective employees, and investors.
- Review local country advertising, packaging, and web content to ensure global brand consistency.

Success Factors

Successful corporate brand marketers have an insatiable thirst for understanding the factors that define consumer brand relationships. They can distill a 100 page report into a handful of critical insights to inform the brand strategy. They are also great communicators, and able to clearly and succinctly articulate the brand strategy to senior executives, and other brand stakeholders.

As with other marketing roles, you will need to work collaboratively with many people and be able to effectively direct the ad agency, marketing communications, and others to execute your program. Importantly, you will need to prove that your strategy is 'working' by implementing (with market research) quantitative surveys that measure changes in consumer brand awareness and perceptions.

Typical Work Week

· Prepare for brand campaign presentation at the national sales meeting

· Meet with market research to discuss brand positioning focus group findings

· Present brand positioning and design standards to new marketing hires

· Update the digital marketing team on the new corporate brand campaign

· Review new brand logo design recommendations
· Meet with the European brand team to review the global brand equity study results
· Meet with the ad agency to review new advertising campaign ideas

Career Path and Salaries

There are many paths to a Corporate Brand Management career, but it's unlikely you'll find an entry-level position. Corporate brand managers usually come up through the ranks of marketing—brand- product management, advertising, and marketing communications. Corporate

brand directors are also recruited from outside the company, often the strategic planners from ad agencies, and brand consultancies. Industry-specific knowledge, while helpful, is not necessarily a key factor in the hiring decision. More important is having the ability to deeply assess customer brand perceptions, and identify unique and differentiating insights that 'connect' with consumers and distinguish it from the competition.

Corporate Brand Directors can expect to earn $150k - $200k plus a 25 - 30% bonus (at companies with $1B + revenue).

Job Outlook

While there is no data specific to job growth for Corporate Brand Management, the proliferation of digital channels (websites, digital media, social media, mobile, etc.) has greatly expanded brand responsibilities. So, employer demand for these roles should remain solid.

Pros/Cons

Pros

- You have an important role in the organization that matters.
- This is both a 'right brain/left brain' role requiring

strategic and creative thinking.
- You work with smart and highly creative people.
- The results of your work can be seen by millions of people.
- It's interesting work, exploring current and future societal, cultural, and consumer psychology trends.
- Employment prospects are good.
- The pay is usually very good.

Cons
- It's a specialized role, focusing on a narrow portion of marketing.
- The job requires lots of 'internal selling' to gain endorsement of the strategy throughout the company.
- The job can require long hours and frequent travel.
- There are a lot of 'cooks in the kitchen', all with different opinions about the brand strategy. Your work is always being critiqued and challenged.
- This is usually not a career path to the C-Suite.

Success Factors
Skills Required
- Strong strategic planning aptitude
- Solid quantitative aptitude
- Deep understanding of qualitative and quantitative market research
- Superior writing and verbal communication skills
- Strong organizational skills
- Superior understanding of brand strategy and positioning

Competencies Required
- Strong leadership skills
- Superior interpersonal skills
- Solid 'creative thinking' abilities

- Superior 'self-starter' requiring limited supervision
- Strong 'team player'
- Strong influencing skills

Landing Your First Job

Corporate brand management is not an entry-level position. It's essential that you first cut your teeth in a Brand, Product, or Advertising management role to learn the fundamentals of brand strategy and brand positioning. You'll need at least 10 years of solid related experience before you would be considered to lead Corporate Brand Management at a major company.

The Bottom Line

Corporate Brand Management is a great career option for people who are strategic and creative. The concept of a 'brand strategy' is not readily understood or appreciated by non-marketers. However, the impact a great corporate brand director can have on the value of the company is significant.

In this section, we'll discuss key roles that plan and execute marketing campaigns:

· Digital Marketing (Campaign) Management
· Integrated Marketing Communication Management
· Demand Generation Management

Marketing campaigns drive trial and repeat purchases of a brand by targeting and influencing consumers via advertising, social media, consumer promotion, shopper marketing, events, and product sampling, among others.

Campaign management roles are akin to that of an 'orchestra conductor'. They create a 'symphony' of coordinated campaign tactics that synergistically work together to find, engage, and motivate the target audience.

Digital Marketing Campaign Manager (DMMs)
Similar Titles:: Omni Channel Manager

The Digital Marketing Manager supports overall brand marketing objectives and strategies by leading the planning, execution, and measurement of an integrated suite of digital communication tactics. Although the digital marketing manager does not need to be an expert in 'all things digital', they are expected to know how to leverage digital media and technology to work synergistically to reach, engage and influence customers.

Digital marketing campaigns are generally comprised of search, advertising, website, e-mail, mobile, and social media channels.

Based on their knowledge of their target audience's online behavior, the manager creates an integrated plan intended to result in having the various tactics work synergistically towards the singular digital campaign goal. To do this, the manager must consider such things as 'how can I find potential customers online? 'which search terms (keywords) do they use when researching a product'? 'what ad copy will motivate them to 'click' and visit the website'? 'what web content will effectively engage them and drive interest in the product'? 'how should the brand's website experience complement the social media program?', among many others.

Job profiles for digital marketing managers vary widely based on the industry and company structure. The following reviews a prototypical digital marketing manager role within a consumer goods company.

Typical Job Description
- Develop integrated digital marketing campaigns supporting the overall brand marketing objectives.
- Lead the development of digital tactics including 'owned' (website, e-mail, mobile), 'earned' (social media), and 'paid' (ads, Google AdWords, etc.) media.
- Establish measurement objectives for the overall digital campaign as well as key performance indicators for digital tactics including search marketing, website visitor & engagement, and e-mail response rates.
- Lead in-depth market research to understand consumer digital behaviors to inform the appropriate digital communication strategy.
- Be a 'thought leader' in emerging media channels, vendors, tools, technology, and best practices. Identify and activate 'next generation' digital pilot programs.
- Use A/B and multivariate testing to relentlessly optimize

campaign performance.

Typical Work Week

- Review new website design and navigation options
- Present next quarter's digital marketing campaign plan to the Marketing VP
- Meet with the marketing technology vendor to review the new e-mail marketing platform capabilities
- Meet with Google AdWords and Facebook sales representatives to review new digital and social media advertising programs
- Review A/B testing plans for alternative campaign landing page designs
- Analyze search ranking results of recent content enhancements
- Review the digital marketing metrics 'dashboard' for this quarter
- Meet with market research to design a web customer journey research study

Career Path and Salaries

Digital marketing managers can pursue two career paths. One path remains specialized in digital marketing and can lead to digital marketing director, and vice president roles. The other path sees the digital marketing manager pivot to brand-product marketing roles.

In my opinion, the latter is the smarter option since deep digital experience is essential to 21st-century marketing. There are many 'old guard' marketers currently occupying the coveted senior management roles. Most have not had the opportunity to learn the complexities of digital marketing. With digital rapidly becoming the 'core' of marketing, your digital expertise will position you well for future senior-level marketing positions.

Salaries

Digital Marketing Managers can expect to earn $80k - $130k + 25 - 30% bonus.

Job Outlook

While there are no statistics about future job growth specifically for digital marketing, these roles are in great demand by employers, and will likely remain so in the future.

Pros/Cons

Pros

- Digital has redefined the profession of marketing forever
- It's interesting and dynamic work, enabling you to consistently grow as a professional
- The job combines 'strategic', 'creative' and 'tech'
- You work with a variety of highly talented people
- There is significant potential for career advancement
- The impact of your work is very measurable
- The pay is good (and getting better)

Cons

- Some companies still do not fully value digital, and thus limit investment
- The job can be highly stressful at times
- There are frequently long hours required
- Digital budgets still lag traditional marketing budgets

Success Factors

Digital marketing managers must have a deep understanding of marketing campaign planning, digital and social media channels, and related technologies. Essential is the ability to collaborate with a wide variety of people. The best DMMs work side-by-side with their brand or product marketing colleagues and are considered invaluable team members. They can translate highly technical digital jargon into clear and simple language that senior management immediately understands

Skills

- Solid business planning and analytical aptitude
- Solid analytical skills
- Solid understanding of traditional and digital marketing communication channels
- Strong understanding of digital marketing technology platforms
- Strong project management and prioritization skills
- Solid abilities as a 'creative problem solver'
- Excellent written and oral communication skills

Competencies

- Solid influencing skills
- Superior ability to multi-task and manage multiple priorities
- Strong interpersonal and collaboration capabilities
- 'Intuitive' grasp of consumer use of digital media and technologies

Landing Your First Job

Normally there are two routes to digital marketing management, each requiring different levels of digital experience. One route is to make a lateral move in your company from a sales, marketing, or analytics job. In your current role, build a reputation for being 'tech savvy', and cultivate relationships with colleagues in the digital marketing department. If you are a 'digital native', who grew up in the world of smartphones and social media, demonstrate this deep knowledge to others when the occasions present themselves. Let it be known that you hope to work in digital marketing and 'get on the radar screen' of HR and the digital marketing department.

As you prepare to interview for a digital marketing entry-level job, conduct your own analysis of the company's digital presence. During the interview, comment on 'what's good', and 'what can be improved' to demonstrate your command of contemporary social, website, and mobile communication channels.

The other route is to seek an entry-level job within an ad agency or a client-side company. This approach will require you to demonstrate some level of experience in digital marketing. You can gain such experience by working on a website for a local business, your school, or a nonprofit. As mentioned in the Demand Generation section, you should consider getting 'certified' in one or more specialized areas of digital marketing such as search marketing, programmatic advertising, digital analytics, and marketing automation. The following companies offer no-cost training for skills that are in demand by employers:

- GROW WITH GOOGLE
- META/FACEBOOK BLUEPRINT
- SALESFORCE TRAILHEAD
- MEDIAMATH ACADEMY
- HUBSPOT ACADEMY

HubSpot notes that people with their certifications get 6 times more views on their LinkedIn profile pages (http://academy.hubspot.com/certification-overview).

The Bottom Line

The Digital Marketing Manager of today should be the Chief Marketing Officer of tomorrow. Digital media and technology are significantly changing each of the '4Ps' of marketing. Progressive companies fully realize the potential of digital to reshape their product innovation, drive customer demand, uncover unique customer & market insights, and enter new distribution channels. Marketing continues to be redefined by rapid advancements in digital. The digital marketing manager role places you at the forefront of the profession.

The objective of every marketing role is to create customer demand for a product. But the term Demand Generation (also referred to as Direct Marketing) is used to describe a distinct approach to marketing communication focused on generating customer leads. A lead is a person who has expressed interest in a product by providing their contact information to the company. Creating these leads (generating demand) is the job of marketing, who then pass them to the salesforce to close the sale (customer acquisition).

B2C and B2B industries use the Demand Generation model to market products (and services) not sold at retail outlets, and that are generally more expensive e.g. automobiles, insurance, technology, real estate, etc. Before making a final purchase decision, potential customers conduct a significant amount of online and offline research - a 'decision journey' evaluating, and comparing one brand versus the other.

Many different titles are used to describe Demand Generation roles—Acquisition Marketing, Database Marketing, Lead Nurturing, e-CRM, Loyalty Marketing, Marketing Automation, etc. But we will focus on Lead Generation, and Customer Relationship Management since these two activities form the essence of the discipline, no matter what the title. We'll also review the 'digital cousin' of De

mand Generation—Inbound Marketing—since this career path is rapidly developing.

The two objectives of Demand Generation are 'Customer

Acquisition' and 'Customer Relationship Marketing' (CRM). Customer Acquisition seeks to find qualified sales prospects (Lead Generation) and to maintain an ongoing relationship resulting to a final sale (Lead Nurturing). Once a new customer has been required, Customer Relationship Marketing takes over to build the customer's loyalty, and have them buy the brand over and over again.

Lead Generation Marketing Manager

Related titles include Inbound Marketing Manager, Demand Generation Manager, Performance Marketing Manager, and Conversion Optimization Manager

All those credit card offers you constantly receive are examples of lead generation in the financial services industry. That free consultation to lower your car insurance? That's also lead generation. If you received these offers, it's because you were selected (targeted) via extensive data analysis. You were then sent a specific offer based on your 'profile'—your age, address, income, past purchases, etc. If you replied to the offer by giving your contact information, you then became a sales 'lead'.

A 'lead' is simply a potential buyer who has expressed some interest in a company's products or services. Lead Generation describes the marketing activities used by

companies to 'identify, nurture and convert' this prospect to a sale. The Lead Generation Marketer's job is to:
- find prospective buyers via targeted media (direct mail, tele-sales, direct response ads, digital channels, etc.)
- engage them with marketing communication (e.g., a brochure, a special offer, etc.)
- get their contact information (name, company, title, e-mail address, etc.) through various offers (a free consultation, an industry 'white paper', etc.)
- pass this contact information to the sales force so they

can close the final sale
- support the sales rep by continuing to deliver useful marketing communication to the prospective buyer (known as Lead Nurturing)

The lead generation manager relentlessly measures, analyzes, and optimizes program performance, toward the goal of delivering highly qualified leads to sales and doing so in the most cost-efficient way. Of course, the sales force will ultimately close the final sale, but the lead generation marketer plays the key 'assist' role.

Typical Job Description
- Develop the lead generation strategy supporting new customer acquisitions.
- Develop the customer segmentation strategy utilizing customer data, analytics, and lead scoring to identify high-growth customer segments.
- Develop the marketing communication campaign strategy.
- Create and execute campaign tactics including direct mail, telemarketing, search marketing, digital advertising, blogs, events, website landing pages, and contact forms.
- Design and execute testing and optimization programs including A/B and multivariate testing programs to optimize conversion rates.
- Create lead scoring criteria to ensure that sales receive the most qualified leads.
- Ensure data integrity including database 'cleanliness' and quality.

Typical Work Week
- Meet with product marketing to review the latest product offerings
- Review the prior week's lead generation campaign results, and identify areas for immediate campaign

optimization
- Assess new marketing technology solutions
- Present Loyalty Marketing recommendations to senior management
- Develop a customer segmentation report
- Review the quality of the customer database records
- Review results of the A/B testing program for new landing page design

Career Path and Salaries

Demand Generation careers can take many paths, depending on the industry or company. In certain industries, such as financial services, lead generation, and customer relationship marketing is a core marketing func

tion. Thus, Demand Generation roles can evolve from Manager (managing Lead Generation and/or CRM programs for a single brand) to Director (managing multiple brands) to Marketing VP or even Chief Marketing Officer.

Salaries

Lead generation and CRM managers can expect to earn between $80k - $130k plus a 25 - 30% bonus.

Job Outlook

While there are no statistics related to the future growth of lead generation manager jobs, these roles are in demand and will likely remain so in the future.

Pros/Cons

Pros
- Your impact on the business is significant and quantifiable
- It's a great field if you love data
- Career progression prospects are very good
- Employment is relatively stable
- The pay can be very good

- You'll work with leading-edge marketing technologies
- The field is emerging as an essential marketing function in most industries

Cons

- This field does not offer exposure to other areas of marketing such as product innovation, pricing, and advertising
- The work environment can be very demanding and 'results now' driven

Success Factors

Strong analytical skills are essential any Demand Generation job. Demand Gen marketers must know how to acquire, structure, interpret, and apply customer data to deliver a customized marketing communication presentation—one that motivates the customer to respond and that ultimately delivers sales.

As with all marketing positions, a passion for 'getting inside the head' of the customer separates the 'good' from the 'great' Demand Gen marketers. Data is an important piece of the customer puzzle, but true insight (and thus competitive advantage) combines these 'quantitative' insights with a more 'qualitative' sense of customer needs—their needs, habits, ambitions, fears, and motivations. This combination delivers a highly targeted and personalized experience that maximizes customer response and ROI.

Skills

- Strong strategic thinking capabilities
- Superior analytical and data reporting knowledge
- Solid written and oral communication skills
- Strong project management skills and attention to detail
- Strong knowledge of marketing strategy and digital marketing

- Experience with e-mail and marketing automation platforms
- Strong knowledge of consumer privacy governance and database 'hygiene'

Competencies

- Solid leadership skills
- Solid influencing skills
- Superior ability to multi-task and manage multiple priorities
- Superior ability to work effectively under tight timelines
- Strong collaboration capabilities
- Strong decision-making skills
- Exceptional customer 'curiosity'

Landing Your First Job

Several entry-level jobs can prepare you for a career in Demand Generation. Depending on the company, 'Marketing Analyst', 'Database Analyst', and Customer Service Rep entry-level can each serve as entryways. As you search for your first job, it's essential to highlight your quantitative and analytical skills. Any position that involves data analytics, especially related to sales and/or marketing campaign performance would provide a solid foundation.

Familiarity with any marketing automation platforms such as Salesforce.com, Marketo, Pardot, Adobe, and Hubspot would also position you well for an entry-level role. Consider investing in marketing automation certifi

cation courses offered by Hubspot. Salesforce, or another vendor. Most are free and provide you with a 'certification' to add to your resume.

As you interview for an entry-level job, use your experience as a consumer to demonstrate your understanding of Demand Generation. Be prepared to describe how you became a 'lead' or member of a loyalty marketing program. What tactics did the brand use to influence you? Have they ever sold you a more expensive product (the latest iPhone perhaps?) or influenced you to buy a complementary product (iPhone case, earbuds, etc.)? What did the brand have to do to 'earn' your loyalty? These are the kinds of answers that should impress any potential hiring manager.

Lastly, note that these jobs have various titles such as 'lead generation', 'performance marketing', 'inbound marketing', and 'direct marketing'. So be sure to search each of these title on job boards.

The Bottom Line
Demand Generation marketers will always be in demand (pun intended). If you'd like a balance of strategic and quantitative work, combined with relentlessly optimizing campaign performance, then consider a career in demand generation. The pay is excellent, and it is a route to senior-level jobs.

Related Roles

Inbound Marketing
Marketing automation platforms such as Hubspot and Marketo have led to the development of the 'Inbound Marketing' concept. While the principles of demand generation remain the same, Inbound Marketing focuses on finding and engaging the customers actively researching products online. While traditional lead generation is about reaching 'Out' (Outbound) to prospective buyers with various programs, Inbound Marketing

is about creating search, advertising, and social media marketing programs that bring sales prospects IN - to the brand's website and/or call center. Once on the site, Inbound Marketing seeks to generate and nurture leads to a final sale.

A four stage framework explains objectives of an inbound marketing campaign:

1. The '**Find**' stage uses SEO (search engine optimization) and SEM (paid search ads) to find people doing online research about a product, and then direct them to the brand's website.

2. The '**Engage**' stage is about providing the potential customer with useful,
    informative, and 'engaging' content to build
    their interest in the brand.

3. The '**Conver**t' stage is focused on securing the
sale, either by creating a customer 'lead' or through an immediate online purchase.

   4. The '**Retain**' stage focuses on buildging brand loyalty of existing customers.

Inbound Marketing positions have many job titles but perform essentially the same function: 'Digital Demand Generation Manager', 'Digital Lead Generation Manager' as well as 'Inbound Marketing Manager' are the most common job titles.

Loyalty Marketing Manager

This primary goal of loyalty marketing is to maximize lifetime customer value by
ensuring that existing customers keep buying the brand. Loyalty marketing uses a variety of techniques to achieve this goal, and to encourage them to buy additional products. 'Cross-selling' complimentary products e.g. adding AppleCare to a MacBook purchase, and 'up-selling' customers to buy a more premium-priced product e.g. upgrading to an iPhone 14 Pro, are

also examples of loyalty marketing.

What's so special about retaining existing customers? Acquiring new customers is very expensive due to the heavy investments in advertising and promotion required to build awareness of the brand, and to influence the customer's first purchase. This often requires the brand to lose money in the short term. It is much more profitable to retain existing customers because the large investment in mass marketing tactics are no longer necessary.

The backbone of loyalty marketing is the customer database. These data power email, direct mail, and telemarketing programs which require very little investment by the brand. Customer databases include such information as the customer's name, home address, email address, and phone number in addition to their prior purchase history. The databases of leading loyalty marketers go far beyond these data points and can include robust 'demographics' (income, education, hobbies, lifestyle interests, family size, etc.), 'psychographic' data (attitudes and opinions about society, politics, religion, etc.), as well as 'behavioral' data (purchases of other products, online versus in-store shopping habits, how frequently products are purchased, etc.

Loyalty marketers lead strategic planning and execution of loyalty programs by utilizing customer data to develop highly customized and targeted tactics. These tactics include 'rewards' programs (e.g., Starbucks Rewards), special promotions, and personalized offers. The loyalty marketer needs a deep understanding of how data is structured, and how to analyze it. While the loyalty marketer does not need a technology background, the role does require a solid understanding of database and marketing automation technologies.

Digital is the dominant channel for Loyalty Marketing, given the low cost of producing and sending email and mobile messaging programs. Refer to the 'Consumer Promotion' and 'Marketing Automation' sections for more information about job responsibilities and career paths.

MARKETING EXECUTION

The following section outlines primaryand related roles responsible for planning and executing specialized areas of marketing programs.

Advertising & Media
Advertising Management
Digital Media Management

Social Media
Social Media Strategy Manager
Social Media Community Manager

Creative and UX/UI Design
User Experience Management
User Interface Management
Graphic Designer

Content Marketing
Content Marketing Strategist

Marketing Automation
Marketing Automation Management

Search Engine Marketing
Search Engine Optimization (SEO) Management
Paid Search (SEM - Search Engine Marketing)

Promotion
Consumer Promotion Management
Shopper Marketing
Trade Marketing

ADVERTISING AND MEDIA CAREERS

Advertising Management

Advertising is about creating memorable and compelling messages that make a brand stand out in this cluttered media landscape. With the average person exposed to over 5,000 ad messages per day, and with the massive proliferation of digital and social channels, competition for consumer "mindshare" has never been greater.

Digital has, and has not, impacted the profession of advertising:
- **What Has Not Changed**: great advertising is grounded in finding unique and compelling insights into consumer needs and desires. These insights form the foundation of original, compelling, and creative messages.
- **What Has Changed**: Everything else...... Digital has radically altered ad targeting, vastly proliferated available media channels, and revolutionized advertising measurement and analytics.

This book will provide the 'client-side' view of advertising—the management of an in-house staff of advertising specialists or outside ad agencies. As noted, this profession typically focuses on the top of the 'Marketing Funnel' to create brand 'awareness' and 'consideration' via TV, print, radio, outdoor and digital channels. We will focus on two core positions—Advertising Manager (Director) and Media Manager (Director).

Job Responsibilities

The advertising manager is responsible for leading the planning, creation, execution, and measurement of the brand's 'integrated' advertising program. 'Integrated' means the holistic planning of the various forms of advertising—TV, print, digital, outdoor, radio, etc. All these channels must work together, synergistically, to have the greatest influence in the overcrowded world of ad messages.

Advertising Managers lead a team of specialists to conceive, create, and distribute great advertising. They first write the advertising brief that directs the activities of the advertising creative, production, and media teams. A lot is riding on the accuracy and clarity of this brief – What is the primary advertising campaign objective? Whom is the advertising intended for? What is the key message to deliver to them? Which product features and benefits should be highlighted? What are the quantifiable advertising goals, and what level of investment is needed to achieve them?

Based on the above information, the ad manager will brief the ad agency to develop the creative strategy. The advertising manager will then review the agency's proposal, and use several criteria to evaluate them – Is the creative idea 'on strategy'? Is there a 'big idea' that will make the ad stand out in the market? Will the ad 'connect' with the target audience, and be remembered and convince them to buy the product? Will the campaign 'have legs' and be able to work far into the future?

The advertising manager will also review the media plan considering a variety of factors. These include evaluating the 'media mix' and how the budget is allocated across various types of media such as network TV, cable TV, print, social media, digital, etc. The ad manager will also assess the plan's 'reach' and 'frequency' which indicate how many times the intended target audience will see the ad, and how often.. Finally, the cost-efficiency of the media plan will be evaluated to get the most media impact for the available budget.

Advertising managers also measure the impact of the advertising, working with the market research team. Finally, they need to 'sell' the advertising program to a variety of people within their company, most importantly the Chief Marketing Officer. This is not always an easy task!

Typical Job Description
- Lead the planning of integrated advertising campaigns in support of overall marketing objectives.
- Manage the in-house (or external advertising agency) to plan, create and execute advertising campaigns, ensuring all work is 'on strategy'.
- Lead the ad agency to develop the campaign's 'big creative idea'.
- Direct the media team to develop cost=effective and innovative programs to reach consumers with the right message, at the right time, in the right place.
- Gain the approvals of advertising concepts by senior management, legal, and other company stakeholders.
- Manage production of audio-visual (video/film/photo) shoots relating to brand and advertising campaigns.
- Lead the planning of advertising and media measurement research.
- Manage budgets for ad production, media, and research.

Typical Work Week
· Attend Product Marketing launch plan meeting
· Meet with an advertising account executive to review ad copy testing results
· Review talent reel to find brand spokesperson for TV ads
· Meet with Facebook sales rep to review new social media ad programs
· Receive a debrief from the media team on media performance
· Lead a team workshop to analyze new cultural trends

· Review production estimate for upcoming TV ad shoot
· Prep for tomorrow's new campaign update to the Marketing VP

Career Path and Salaries

Typically, a client-side advertising manager has some ad agency work experience. It's also a specialized area of marketing so the career path is relatively limited. An advertising manager (responsible for a single brand or area

of the business) can move to advertising director or VP, managing advertising for a portfolio of brands, or even the entire company. They can also move into marketing management positions (Brand or Product management) since advertising skills provide an ideal foundation.

Salaries

Salaries vary significantly depending on the size of the company, but Advertising Managers at large companies can expect to earn between $80k - $120k plus a 20 - 25% bonus.

Job Outlook

There is no specific data for advertising management job growth. However, the job outlook for digital advertising experience will certainly be robust for many years.

Success Factors

A great advertising manager is truly a 'left brain' / 'right brain' person. They need to be able to judge creativity, but also be comfortable digging into analytics. They need to 'relate' to, and motivate a cast of characters ranging from creative directors to copywriters to media planners to video producers. Being a good 'salesperson' to gain buy-in for ad programs is also very helpful. The campaign idea goes nowhere unless executive management gives the green light. Most importantly, a great advertising manager has an insatiable thirst to find "the big idea" and that special 'connection' to the customer. Discovering unique insights into their unspoken needs and motivations is the 'secret sauce' of exceptional advertising.

Skills Required
· Strong strategic thinking capabilities
· Superior ability to assess ad creative concepts
· Deep understanding of brand strategy and positioning
· Strong project management skills
· Superior written and verbal communication skills

Competencies Required
· Strong leadership skills
· Superior influencing skills
· Ability to multi-task and manage multiple priorities

Pros/Cons
Pros
- A highly visible and important role in most companies
- The most 'creative' of all marketing roles
- Millions of people see the results of your work every day
- You work with a vast array of different kinds of people
- The pay can be very good

Cons
- The job is frequently very stressful
- Everyone has an opinion about your work
- There can be long hours during key periods
- Employment security can sometimes be unpredictable
- This is not usually a path to executive management
- Work-life balance can frequently be challenging

Landing Your First Job
If advertising management appeals to you as a career option, you should pursue both

client-side and agency-side opportunities. There is no cookie-cutter approach to activating an advertising career, and the industry is notoriously difficult to land an entry-level job. The glamour of advertising attracts many of the best and brightest who are competing for a handful of these low-paying jobs. Look for any type of entry position, whether it be a media, research, or even administrative role. This is frequently the first step in the advertising management career journey.

Effective networking is the key to landing your first job. You will need to aggressively find other alumni, friends, neighbors, or others to help secure an 'informational interview' at an ad agency or company. Target your efforts by reading *Ad Age* and other industry publications: Which brands are investing in new advertising campaigns? Which agencies are getting new business? Who are the people leading the campaign at the client and agency?

Once you have secured an interview, it's very important to articulate your motivations for pursuing this career and how your experiences and skills position you for success. You must become a 'student' of great advertising

and marketing. Constantly critique the ads you see on TV, in magazines, or online: What was the goal of the advertising? What was the 'big idea' in the ad? (Was there even a 'big idea'?) Who is the intended target audience? What was the key ad message and was it memorable? Having a well-considered point of view should give you a leg-up in landing your first job.

The Bottom Line
Advertising is a fascinating profession at the intersection of consumer psychology and creative expression. It's a competitive field, and one that's frequently all-consuming. But this role has a tremendous influence on the success of the brand, and the fruits of your labor will be seen by millions.

(Digital) Media Management

Most media jobs reside in ad agencies or media buying agencies. Client-side media career opportunities usually only exist at companies that invest heavily in advertising. These client-side Media Managers are responsible for planning and executing media for some or all the brands within the company. They will work with the product or brand manager to define their media objectives, the intended target audience, the budget, timing, etc.

A key responsibility of media management is planning the 'media mix' (the various types of media), and how the budget is allocated across each type. Media managers set objectives for the campaign's 'reach' and 'frequency', to ensure that the target audience is sufficiently exposed to the ad message. The manager also assesses the 'quality' and reputation of the media properties being considered, and evaluates the cost efficiency of the media plan to get the most ad exposure for the available budget.

Media management has changed radically with the emergence of the digital era. In the old days, a typical media program consisted of television advertising, some print advertising, and perhaps a smattering of radio and outdoor advertising. There is now an overwhelming number of media channels (e.g., mobile and social) and formats (e.g., online video) for the advertiser to consider. Digital has also ushered in an entirely new era using highly sophisticated approaches such as social media,

programmatic, behavioral, remarketing, and 'contextual' advertising.

New and specialized digital media roles are becoming increasingly common. Some of these roles are focused on specific digital channels including Social Media advertising. The **Social Media Advertising Manager** plans and executes paid advertising on Facebook, Tiktok, Instagram, etc. As social media's importance in the marketing mix continues to grow, we can expect to see a large increase in demand for this specialized role.

Programmatic advertising now dominates digital display media investment. The **Programmatic Advertising Manager** plans and executes campaigns that target 'audiences', with digital ads, served across thousands of websites using sophisticated 'demand-side platforms' (DSP's). This highly sophisticated model uses artificial intellignce to micro-target ads to very specific audiences e.g. 'to people who earn over $100k per year, have large families, like cooking, are religious and active in their local community politics'. Programmatic also uses real-time bidding so thousands of publishers (websites) instantly bid for the right to serve the ad on their website, thus driving down the cost of advertising for a brand.

Other new, and increasingly in-demand roles include the **Digital Ad Optimization Specialist** and **Digital Media Analytics Specialist**. These are also 'hot jobs' focused on analyzing advertising performance across all digital

channels, including paid search, programmatic, and social media advertising.

Companies with client-side media jobs almost always recruit people with several years of experience, usually from an ad agency. Thus, it's highly unlikely you will be able to begin a digital media career at a client-side company. But for those with agency experience, a career shift to a client-side position has many benefits including higher pay and greater job security.

If you are keen to pursue this field, begin by exploring entry-level roles at advertising agencies. Many of the top agencies recruit people with no experience, but who demonstrate analytical and managerial potential.

Search Engine Marketing Management

There are over one billion websites in the world and over 1.5 trillion web searches per year. Within this vast digital universe, brands compete every day for the attention of prospective buyers. Search engine marketing management is the 'art' and 'science' of influencing search engine page rankings, enabling a brand or company to be listed ahead of competitors on the most popular search engines—namely Google.

There are two sub-specializations in search engine marketing management:
- Search Engine Marketing (SEM), also known as 'Paid Search' and 'Sponsored Search'. This role focuses on plan

ning and executing paid search advertisements that appear above and/or alongside search results

- Search Engine Optimization (SEO), also known as 'Organic Search' or 'Natural Search'. SEO focuses on improving the ranking of a webpage within the 'free' search results that appear on the search results page.

Both SEM and SEO work towards the same goals - to secure top ranking in search queries, and to influence the customer to 'click' and visit a web page. There is no fee paid for a visit to a brand web page from an organic search. However, the link to the page may be buried many pages deep in the search results. With SEM, the brand pays for their ad to appear on the first page of the search engine, and pays a fee each time a person clicks on it.

Search Engine Marketing (SEM) Manager

Similar Titles: Paid Search Manager, PPC Manager, Google AdWords Specialist

The Search Engine Marketing Manager is responsible for developing and implementing targeted 'paid' search marketing campaigns on the leading search engines towards the ultimate goal of maximizing website traffic. The SEM Manager will develop the 'keyword strategy'. This determines the words and phrases a prospective customer might enter into a search engine when researching a product. The manager then creates the copy for the paid ads that are displayed in the search results. The next step is to set the 'bidding' criteria for each of

these keywords i.e. the amount of money the brand is willing to pay when someone clicks on the ad.

Search engines use a variety of criteria to determine which advertiser gets top placement. These include the amount of the bid, the quality of the ad, and how relevant the content on the brand's web page is to the consumer's search query. The SEM manager needs to consider each these when designing the program.

Continuous measurement and optimization are essential responsibilities. The manager will continually evaluate consumer responsiveness to the ads to improve overall program performance – Which ads were clicked? What was the 'click-through rate'? (the number ad clicks divided by the number of times it was displayed)? What lessons were learned to inform the keyword strategy and copy used in the ads?

This is a sought-after role and critical to the success of many small and large companies. If you are highly competitive, love data, and have a relentless passion for continuous improvement, then Search Marketing could be a great career option.

Typical Job Description

- Plan and execute paid search (SEM) initiatives in support of overall brand or company marketing objectives including national and geo-targeted campaigns in the leading search engines.
- Define campaign goals, key target audiences, search keywords, ad copy, and click bid amounts (the maximum amount the brand is willing to pay per click).
- Work collaboratively with the website manager and copywriters to plan and develop SEM-optimized landing pages.
- Ensure web page content is relevant to the consumer's search query.
- Set up, schedule, and implement national and local geo-targeted campaigns in key primary (Google, Yahoo! and MSN) and secondary search engines.
- Leverage all of the targeting tools available by the search engine to maximize campaign results.
- Monitor and continually optimize bids to maximize campaign ROI.
- Frequently analyze and modify targeting, keyword, and bid criteria.

Success Factors

Great search engine marketers are relentless optimizers. They 'think' like a shopper, and consider which keywords best align with the prospective customer's 'purchase decision journey'. What might someone type into the Google search bar when they are in the early stages of researching a new television purchase? What might they search for when they are now ready to purchase it? How can they divert traffic away from a competitor's website? Of course, strong search engine marketers love getting deep into the data and are never satisfied. They are always striving for the perfect campaign.

Skills

- Superior knowledge of leading search engine SEM programs including Google AdWords and BingAds
- Strong analytical skills and ability to draw conclusions and determine strategies based on data
- Superior financial management and budgeting skills
- Solid oral, written, and interpersonal communication skills

Competencies

- Solid influencing skills
- Superior ability to multi-task and manage multiple priorities
- Strong interpersonal and collaboration capabilities
- 'Intuitive' grasp of digital media and related technologies

Search Engine Optimization (SEO) Manager

Similar Titles: SEO Specialist, SEO Coordinator, or SEO Strategist

The Search Engine Optimization Manager is an important, albeit back-office role in most organizations. One part 'content manager' and another part 'technical', the SEO manager is responsible for ensuring that links to a brand website index (rank) as high as possible in search engine 'organic' (free) search listings.

Sophisticated algorithms are used by search engines to interpret consumer search queries. These algorithms

have only one goal—to deliver to the person searching a list of the most accurate and unbiased web pages that will best match the query. There are many criteria that determine search engine ranking, many of which cannot be influenced by the SEO manager. However, they can influence ranking by managing three critical factors: content, tagging, and backlinks.

The SEO Manager ensures that the content on a website is written in an 'SEO friendly' manner. Thus, they ensure that the content on each webpage considers the most likely keywords that could trigger a search for the information on that page. Tagging refers to placing simple code on web pages that 'tell' the search engine what information on them. Backlinks are links to a brand's web pages by other websites. These are an important ranking criteria used by the search engines, so the SEO manager works to maximize the number of these links (URL).

Typical Job Description
- Develop the search engine optimization strategy.
- Assess competitive search results and developing the brand's primary keyword list and content, meta-tagging, technical, and backlinking strategies.
- Establish SEO targets, monitor results, and report regularly.
- Establish a scorecard to measure changes in keyword search rankings.
- Develop detailed keyword and linking strategies for optimal SEO performance.
- Select keywords that best meet the information needs of the customer.
- Work closely with the website manager and SEM manager to inform web content and coordinate fully integrated search campaigns.
- Ensure that website pages contain the required keywords and meta-tags.
- Be a 'thought leader' in search optimization trends and best practices.
- Continually monitor changes to the search engine algorithms and adjust the SEO strategy accordingly.

Success Factors
SEO managers must 'think' like a shopper to plan keywords

based on the customer's 'purchase decision journey'. SEO managers convert this insight into specific website content and page-tagging recommendations that optimize search ranking. Great managers are relentlessly optimizing—there is no goal line in SEO.

Skills
· Deep knowledge of search engines ranking criteria
· Strong analytics skills
· Solid strategic thinking capabilities
· Knowledge of HTML, Google Analytics, and Webmaster tools
· Strong experience with SEO Tools such as SEOMoz
· Strong project management skills
· Solid oral and written communication skills

Competencies
· Solid interpersonal skills

· Solid ability to work collaboratively
· Solid influencing skills
· Ability to multi-task and manage multiple priorities

Pros/Cons
Pros
- SEO is a dynamic, ever-changing field
- The work is highly quantifiable
- You work with smart people across the organization
- The job provides a solid foundation for other digital marketing careers
- Good job security
- Limited, if any travel
- Strong potential to work as an independent consultant

Cons
- It's a very specialized role that can be considered 'behind the scenes'
- Good but not great pay

- There are many factors impacting search rankings that are out of your control

Career Path

The success (or failure) of many companies depends on their ability to find and prospective customers doing online research. As such, search marketing is an essential ingredient in the marketing mix. SEM skills are in great demand now and will certainly be well into the future. Search Engine Marketing can be a lucrative career path on the client side, in an ad agency, or as an independent

contractor. Also, if you have ambitions to move up within client-side companies, an SEM background will serve as a great foundation for moving into a Digital Marketing Manager role.

SEO careers are perhaps the most specialized in marketing. In most client-side companies, search engine optimization is considered more of a 'back office' type role and would not be a good platform for future career growth. However, you have significant potential to develop your career with ad agencies, search consulting firms, or as an independent consultant.

Salaries

SEM Managers can expect to earn $60k - $100k + a 25 - 30% bonus. SEO Managers can expect to earn $60k - $100k.

Job Outlook

While no data exists, SEO and SEM job opportunities are likely to increase in the years ahead.

Landing Your First Job

Your first job will require some basic training in search marketing, but the leading search engines provide extensive and free training to learn SEM.

Through Google, you can immediately begin your SEM training with their AdWords Certification program (https://

support.google.com/partners/answer/3154326?hl=en). Here you will find complete instructions and extensive online study guides. You will need to pass the Adwords fundamental exam, as well as

one of five other exams (Search Advertising, Display Advertising, Mobile Advertising, Video Advertising, or Shopping Advertising). There is no certification offered by Google for SEO, but there are many resources available from Google, other search engines, and community forums.

For those interested in pursuing a search marketing career, I would suggest getting certified by Google and then getting as much 'desk training' as possible. Get some hands-on experience actually managing SEO or SEM for a website. Many small business owners and/or non-profit groups would likely jump at the chance to have someone apply this knowledge to improve their site traffic. Some volunteer experiences would go a long way to opening doors for a full-time role.

The Bottom Line

Search marketing is a great career option for those seeking a highly specialized role that focuses on the psychology of why and how people search online. This career also has excellent job security, good pay, and the ability to work at a company or as an independent contractor.

WEBSITE COMMUNICATION MANAGEMENT

Similar Titles: Web Communication or Web Experience Manager

Delivering a great website experience is a hugely challenging, yet ultimately rewarding career opportunity. Your work helps millions of people find valuable product information to support their purchase decision, to help them troubleshoot or fix a product, and to inform them about your company. You are not just promoting, you are publishing. There are vast opportunities for both strategic and creative fulfillment in Web Communication Management.

A website is a brand's or company's digital storefront, and first impressions matter—A LOT. A second-rate website leaves the impression that the company is also second-rate. The website design, layout, and content speak volumes about the quality of the company, its products, and the people that work there. What does it say about your company if a customer struggles to find even the basic information they're looking for? Or if the content they find is incomplete or poorly written?

Many specialized positions revolve around the website—UX (user experience), web design, information architecture, content strategy, front-end development, analytics, back-end development, etc. Similar to a great symphonic orchestra, each plays a critical role. Web Communication Management serves as the conductor of the site experience to publish a work of art and utility.

Website Communication Manager

The website serves as the central 'hub' of the digital marketing mix, with all roads (digital ads, e-mail, social media, search) leading to it. The website communication manager is responsible for the overall planning and implementing this 'experience' to influence purchase by delivering a satisfying and compelling customer 'experience'.

Brand websites serve two masters, the site visitor (your customer or prospective customer) and the brand. A website that serves as nothing more than a digital version of your advertising will provide little value to the visitor—and they will quickly exit your site. On the other hand, a website that simply entertains visitors without 'selling' is a poor business investment. The website manager sits at the intersection of these two (not incompatible) objectives.

The fay to day work of a web communication manager involves publishing brand content, fixing technical issues, and planning new upgrades to the site experience. These upgrades might include a new site design, or adding new 'functionality' such as an interactive game, integrating social media, adding audio-visual tools, etc.

About every two or three years you will likely be leading a major upgrade of the entire website platform. This determining what specific upgrades required (the 'site requirements'). Perhaps the marketing department is seeking to grow its e-mail database and needs the website to

collect consumer contact information. Or maybe a brand needs to showcase their latest product with cool ways to display photos and videos. The manager will work with the brand or product manager to define these requirements. With this information the web communication manager will apply their knowledge of the latest technology and web design to create a web experience that delights customers and influences sales.

Unlike the well-defined roles within traditional marketing, website manager roles can reside in any one of several departments including marketing, IT, or another corporate function. No matter where it resides in the company, this is first and foremost a marketing-based role.

Job Responsibilities

- Develop the overall website strategy.
- Define requirements for creating the optimal site user experience including website design, information architecture strategy, content, and functionality.
- Lead the editorial planning and publishing of web content through the web content management system.
- Define, measure, and report website goals including user satisfaction, site traffic, site engagement, and conversion.
- Partner with the IT organization to define next-generation website platform enhancements enabling the website to remain best-in-class.
- Ensure the brand is presented in a premium and consistent way globally.
- Be a thought leader in digital and provide recommendations to consistently drive website innovation.

Typical Work Week

- Check the latest web content and application updates made to the website
- Meet with the editorial team to plan content for holiday promotion
- Review the new homepage design options with the ad agency
- Meet with Information Technology Director, to discuss the new mobile website
- Debrief from the brand team on new product launch and website requirements
- Review new site visitor satisfaction survey results. Discuss optimization plans
- Conduct a final review of new landing pages and push live to the website

- Attend the 'Marketing Technology Trends' webinar
- Work on a long-term strategic plan for website enhancements

Career Path

Website Management is a highly specialized career and is not a path to senior marketing management. That said, it offers an excellent opportunity to grow as a professional. You will be at the forefront of digital technology that is transforming virtually every industry. You will work

with a lot of smart people with varied backgrounds and see every day (along with millions of other people) the results of your work.

As a web manager, you will learn many of the key skills of 21st-century marketing. Moving laterally into a digital marketing manager position is a likely avenue for further career progression. You would also have the opportunity to work in an agency or consulting role. Websites will forever serve as the digital 'hub', and these skills will remain in high demand.

Salaries

Web Communication Manager salaries vary greatly and range between $60k - $130k plus a 15% - 30% bonus. However, the pay at large companies can be significantly higher.

Job Outlook

Website Manager job opportunities should continue to grow in the years ahead as companies accelerate investment in their digital transformations.

Success Factors

Web communication managers possess a wide array of skills and competencies. The job requires both strategic thinking and the ability to effectively execute. It also requires strong design and creative instincts, with a knack for technology and analytics. The web manager must wear two hats and think like the customer, as well as a businessperson. They need to manage today's 'real-time' experience on the website while also planning years into

the future. Web Communication Managers are indeed a special breed.

Skills

· Superior understanding of web user experience and technologies
· Strong understanding of digital marketing
· Strong project management skills
· Solid analytical abilities
· Superior ability to lead diverse teams including marketing, technical, and creative
· Solid written and oral communication skills

Competencies

· Solid interpersonal skills. Ability to work collaboratively
· Solid influencing skills
· Superior ability to manage multiple priorities
· Ability to work effectively under tight timelines

Pros / Cons

Pros

- It's both a strategic and creative position
- You will work with leading-edge digital technologies
- It's a dynamic and ever-changing field
- You work with a lot of interesting and smart people
- Your work is 'published' and viewed by millions of people
- Employment is stable with good pay

Cons

- It's a specialized role focusing on just one component of

digital marketing
- The pay is good but lower than other marketing management jobs
- It's not a path to senior management
- The job can be extremely stressful at times

Landing Your First Job

There is no defined entryway, but many paths can lead to a career in website management. Since virtually all digital specialties intersect with the website, experience in search marketing, content development, website analytics, and social media provide solid foundations.

There are many ways to acquire basic website development skills. Simply creating your own website on a topic you are passionate about is a great first step. Also, there are many small businesses and nonprofit organizations that would jump at the chance to have you design and build a better website. Platforms such as Shopify (www.shopify.com) and Hubspot (www.hubspot.com) have excellent, easy, and (relatively) low-cost ready-made platforms that do not require coding experience.

The Bottom Line

For many brands and companies today, the website is the second most important component of the marketing mix, second only to the product or service being sold. As a web communication manager, you will serve two important stakeholders—your site visitors, and your company. You are one part 'publisher' and one part 'marketer', ensuring the website experience serves the customer and the business. The job provides an interesting and dynamic mix of technology, content, consumer behavior, and analytics. How cool is that?

Related Careers

Web Development

Web development is not a marketing role but as a digital marketer, you will be hugely dependent on these talented people to build and operate your website and applications. Below is a basic understanding of the key types of web developers you may be interacting with.

Front-End Development

Front-end development creates the code required to deliver what you see on a webpage. The worldwide web is entirely 'virtual' and every webpage and component of the page is made possible through lines and lines of code. Go to any website using the Chrome browser and click 'control U'. Here you will see the work of the Front-end Developer created with HTML, CSS, JavaScript, and other programming languages. Front-end developers work closely with the Interaction and UX designers and bring the web page 'concepts' to (virtual) life.

Back-End Developer

Back-end developers build, connect, and operate the various technologies (web servers, application servers, databases) that enable this information to be accessed and served to the website visitor. They work in the world

of .Net, Java, PHP, and MySQL and run the engine room that makes this digital thing possible.

Mobile App Developer

Mobile app developers focus on the coding required to 'make what you see' on a smartphone. Similar to websites, they work with interaction designers, information architects, and UX designers to convert these 'concepts' to hard code. While there are many operating systems, the Mobile App Developer will primarily work on the Android (used by Samsung Smartphones) and iOS (used by Apple devices) platforms. Since almost every digital marketing plan now includes a mobile experience, you will certainly be working with these talented people.

Information Architect (IA)

Websites can consist of tens of thousands of pages of information. Information architecture is the art and science of organizing this information to make it as easy as possible for a site visitor to find exactly the information they are looking for. Part of this role involves creating the site map, which specifies each of the various sections of the website, how each section is aligned to one another, and the exact order of web pages within each section. The Information Architect is also responsible for what's called 'taxonomy' which determines how to classify or label website content. This takes thoughtful planning and consideration , and how people search for information on the web.

SOCIAL MEDIA MANAGEMENT

Social media is the most transformative and complex communication medium in history. It brings us together as global citizens while at the same time isolating us in our own private Idaho of cyberspace. It can foster the widespread and immediate distribution of important knowledge, but is mainly used to share rather worthless personal information. It can instantly fuel a peaceful revolution, or be used for public shaming and bullying. These contradictions aside, social media is truly the next frontier for marketers. Marketers who 'get' this new medium will receive great benefits while those that don't will pay an enormous price.

Of course, social media is not just a single media platform like TV and radio. Rather, it is comprised of many different platforms with unique capabilities and characteristics. From a marketing standpoint, social media can be segmented as follows:

- Blogs - such as Huffington Post and TMZ
- Social Networks – such as Facebook, LinkedIn, Google+
- Content Sharing Platforms – such as TikTok, YouTube, Pinterest, Instagram, Snapchat, Vine
- Microblogs – such as Twitter
- Content Aggregation Platforms – such as Mashable, Tumblr

Thankfully, these amazing platforms were not built to accommodate marketers and advertisers. They were

built to serve a greater purpose, adding value to the life of the user. Their application as a marketing platform came after the fact. As such, you will find social media properties that are thriving as marketing platforms while others are struggling.

The marketer needs to ask the question: 'how can social media uniquely help drive my sales?' Marketers don't need yet another medium to deliver a simple ad impression or a coupon. So, a good social media marketing plan will begin by asking the question 'how can social media uniquely contribute to the plan?

There are two unique benefits to social media for a marketer:
· Word of Mouth Marketing - the most potent of all forms of marketing is loyal customers recommending your brand to their social network.
· Highly Targeted Advertising - whereby ads are displayed based on analysis of a person's unique social media profile and interests

When using traditional media, the marketer asks the question: 'what message do I want to deliver to my target audience?' Good marketers DO NOT approach social media in the same manner. Rather, the first question asked is 'what content can I provide to my brand fans that they would find of value and want to share with their social network?'

I could write a book about the fundamental differences between these two questions. But suffice it to say that

there is a new rulebook for social media marketing that's grounded in fresh, progressive thinking. As you consider alternative companies to work for, pressure test which rulebook they are using.

Career opportunities on the client side of marketing include Social Media Manager and Social Media Community Manager roles. The Social Media Manager is the architect of the overall social media strategy, leading its execution and measurement. The Social Media Community Manager represents the 'voice' of the brand (or company), directing the 'conversation' across all social channels. Despite being highly specialized, these jobs offer an excellent opportunity for professional development—and under certain circumstances, excellent career progression.

Social Media Manager

Social Media Managers develop an overarching strategy that coordinates all social media channels to support the larger marketing communication goals. The strategy could focus on driving brand awareness of a new product introduction, identifying sales leads, or foster brand loyalty. The strategy will define the social media goals, the specific audience to be targeted, which social channels will be used and why, as well as the intended content & messaging for each.

People use social media platforms for different purposes. Some platforms provide a 'visually driven' experience e.g., TikTok, YouTube, and Pinterest. Others provide

users with a forum for community discussions e.g. Twitter, Facebook, and blogs. When developing the strategy, the social media manager must define the unique role of each platform in the overall plan. This enables the brand to leverage the strengths of each to more effectively engage their audience.

Once the strategy has been established, the manager will develop a social media 'calendar' that details the content plan. This spells out the specific content that will be posted on each social media platform, on what days and at what times. The manager uses the calendar to direct the production of the specific content (posts, videos, graphics etc.) needed for each platform.

Social media programs take a lot of administrative work. To assist with this, the manager will use a single tool to coordinate the calendar, distribute content, and measure audience engagement. There are many of these tools including Spriklr, Salesforce Studio, and Spredfast.

Social media managers also monitors social channels to gather market and customer insights. The manager will select a 'social listening' platform e.g., Radiona6, and to collect the social 'buzz' i.e. what people are saying about the brand and/or company.

Note – The social media advertising role previously discussed is sometimes an additional responsibility of the Social Media Manager.

Job Responsibilities
- Develop the social media objectives, strategy, and marketing campaign.
- Define key performance indicators for each social media channel.
- Create and maintain social media channels including Facebook, TikTok, Twitter, YouTube, Instagram, Pinterest, and Snapchat.
- Lead the creative team to conceive and create content that is highly shareable and appropriate for specific channels.
- Implement the brand 'social listening' program.
- Serve as the 'thought leader' for future social media trends & technologies.

Typical Work Week
- Scan customer posts across the brand's social channels
- Update the Facebook editorial calendar with the social media community manager
- Review the new YouTube brand channel designs with the creative team
- Write a report summarizing last month's social media performance
- Debrief from Brand team on new product launch and social media goals
- Review Facebook advertising campaign with the ad agency
- Review a new 'social listening' platform with the vendor
- Review activity on competitor social media platforms

Career Path

Social Media is growing by leaps and bounds as a marketing platform and provides excellent career growth potential. That said, it is a highly specialized field. On the 'client side' social media provides a mid-manager level career opportunity. Thus, a social media manager could be promoted to director level and oversee all social media activity within a company.

With several years of experience, you could also work as an independent consultant Companies are increasingly dropping the 'staff-laden' agency model, choosing to outsource specific skills at a fraction of the price. Note that this fraction of the price still pays the independent consultant handsomely.

Salaries

Social Media Manager salaries vary widely and range between $50k - $100k plus a 10 - 20% bonus.

Pros/Cons

Pros

- Your work is in 'real-time' and seen by thousands (or millions) of people
- Social media marketing is a dynamic industry that is constantly being reinvented
- It's 'real-time' marketing that is constantly shifting based on social conversations
- Every day opens new opportunities and challenges
- You work with very young and talented people
- Excellent employment opportunities long term

Cons

- It's a very specialized role that can be considered 'behind the scenes'
- Salaries are good but on the lower end of the marketing pay scale

- It's not a path to senior management
- The job can be very stressful at times
- Often requires irregular working hours including evenings and weekends

Success Factors

As you would expect, all Social Media Managers are masters of all things social. The best managers are strategic thinkers, able to define the unique role of each platform in supporting the overall plan. What's the role of Twitter versus Facebook versus Instagram from a marketing communication standpoint? Which channels reach the most members of my target audience? How should the social media marketing programs be tailored for each channel?

Successful Social Media Managers are also deeply 'in tune' with their audience and pour over hundreds of posts on any given day. These managers are often the most knowledgeable people in the company about consumer trends, competitive activities, and the reputation of the brand. Smart brand and product manager rely on their social media managers as a valuable source of market and consumer insights. Their real-time knowledge makes them very important people in the organization!

Skills and Competencies Required
Skills

- Superior knowledge of major and emerging social media channels including Facebook, Twitter, Instagram, Pinterest, Snapchat, Google+, LinkedIn, TikTok, and YouTube
- Strong project management skills
- Solid analytical abilities
- Strong content and messaging development skills
- Superior written and oral communication skills
- Solid digital marketing and marketing knowledge

Competencies

- Strong interpersonal skills and ability to work collaboratively
- Solid influencing skills
- Superior ability to multi-task and manage multiple priorities
- Superior ability to work effectively under tight timelines

Landing Your First Job

Similar to the guidance provided for an entry level web communication job, find a way to get ANY relevant experience —at your school, a local business, and the not-for-profit group will go a long way. Your prospective hiring manager likely has very limited knowledge of social media. When interviewing, your goal is to impress them with your fluent understanding of how and why their customer use social media. Conduct your own evaluation of their social media program, and identify the 'missed

opportunities'—how can you help them drive deeper engagement for their brand? How should they increase social word-of-mouth marketing? They need you; they just need to know why!

The Bottom Line

Social Media Management is a fascinating role that leads an important element of the marketing strategy. In the past, social media was considered a 'nice to have' component of the marketing mix, taking a back seat to advertising. Today, social media is a central component of the marketing program. Social media managers have an important 'seat at the table' to influence the overall marketing plan. In this role, you will serve as the 'thought leader' for current and future social media opportunities, and be highly valued member of the marketing organization.

Social Media Community Manager
Similar Titles: Social Media Planner, Social Media Coordinator

The Social Media Community Manager is on the 'front time', responsible for managing the 'conversation' across one or more of a brand's social media channels. The work includes viewing, posting, and responding to consumer comments on a daily basis. The role has swiftly become an essential component of brand communication, and typically pays between $35k - $70k.

As discussed in the Demand Generation section, only a handful of 'most valuable customers (MVCs) account for the overwhelming majority of a brand's sales and profits. In social media language, these are called 'brand fans'. An important function of the social media community manager is to engage with this community and nurture these important relationships.

The community manager's work strongly influences consumer perceptions of the brand, arguably even more than advertising. A great community manager speaks within the 'character' of the brand or company but does so in a way that 'connects' with the audience in a genuine and personal manner. The best ones are honest, responsive, and always positive no matter what the situation. This requires a very talented, and often patient person.

Job Responsibilities
The Community Manager works with the social media manager to develop and implement the editorial calendar for a brand's (or company's) social media channels. They also collaborate to plan,

source, and create content including text, photos, videos, and infographics. Daily, the Community Manager posts this content and finds opportunities to 'engage' in real-time conversations with the brand's fans.

An important role of the community manager is to redirect customer inquiries to appropriate departments within the organization. For example, a product complaint would be sent to Customer Service, a job inquiry sent to the HR department, etc. The community manager is also responsible for escalating social media conversations that could have legal, security, or negative brand reputation implications. (There are some crazy people out there with a lot of time on their hands to rant and rave!).

Skills and Competencies Required

Outstanding writing and verbal communication skills are essential, as is an 'intuitive' sense of the 'language' and culture of social conversations. Deep knowledge of digital media and current/emerging social media channels is critical. The community manager must also be able to simultaneously manage multiple priorities.

CONTENT MARKETING

Content Marketing is a relatively new role that leads the creation of content across a brand' digital and non-digital communication channels. The primary purpose is to create a holistic program that delivers a compelling, meaningful, and consistent experience for consumers, wherever and whenever they engage with the brand. A secondary purpose is to reduce costs by centralizing content production.

Many brands are now adopting Omni Channel Marketing which analyzes existing data to deliver more personalized and relevant content to the customer. Omni Channel is grounded in the customer database and the knowledge it holds about an individual customer e.g. their prior purchases, browsing history on the brand's website, e-mail from the brand that they've read, promotions they have signed up for etc.

The goal of Omni Channel is to use this past knowledge to predict what brand or product information would the customer find most useful today. With this insight, the brand is able to deliver that information the next time the customer engages with the website, an e-mail, a salesperson, or a customer service representative.

Retailers are ahead of the curve in applying the Omni Channel model. By way of example, Bloomingdale's database might indicate that an upcoming sale at a local store would likely be of interest to a customer. They could the send an SMS message, and based on the customer's past

wardrobe purchases, highlight complimentary accessories that are on sale. When the customer is in the store, a salesperson would also have access to customer's data, and thus have insights into their taste in fashion. The salesperson could then assist the shopper and make specific recommendations for their purchase. Since the data about customer's new purchase is immediately added to the Bloomingdales central database, the marketing team would then use this information to send customized offers for in-store or online promotions via e-mail.

A lot of content is needed to power an Omni Channel program. Many different formats are needed to serve many different types if customers across many different brand 'touchpoints'. Additionally, Omni Channel is being adopted by more and more marketers. Therefore, the demand for content marketers will certainly continue to grow.

Job Responsibilities

The content marketer manager plans and creates multiple content assets (videos, webpages, social media posts, email messages, etc.) for distribution across online and offline channels. The content created is not purely 'promotional' but also intended to provide customers with information they would find useful for making a better purchase decision.

The content marketing manager 'creates once for distribution to many'. This means that they first consider the complete scope of the digital and non-digital channels

included in the marketing communication plan. They then coordinate the centralized production of all the necessary formats of content at the same time. For example, a single shoot would capture all the video content needed for YouTube (e.g., a 10-minute 'how to' video), digital advertising (e.g., a 30-second spot), and the website (e.g., customer success video). This saves time and money while ensuring that all content maintains a similar creative style.

This job requires many skill sets, most importantly the ability to lead the creation of content that captures the customer's attention and delivers a useful and compelling experience for them. The ability to coordinate a vast team of writers, graphic designers, video producers, etc. across various media formats (video, web, mobile, print) is also important.

Skills and Competencies Required

A successful content management career requires skills in copywriting, editorial planning, and an ability to create content across various digital formats including web pages, blogs, and e-mail. Exceptional organizational skills, and an ability to 'multi-task' and work productively in a deadline-driven environment are also essential. Content managers also need to deep knowledge of digital asset management systems, as well as graphic design applications (such as Canva, Figma, and Adobe Photoshop).

Career Path

Many content managers are not interested in moving into higher positions, preferring to enjoy their role as individual contributors. For those that do want to rise in the ranks, it will usually take two to three years of experience to be promoted and manage a team of content creators (employees as well as freelancers).

Given that 'content is king' for all digital channels, content managers also have the opportunity to pivot to other digital marketing careers, such as web communications, digital production, and social media marketing.

Salaries

Content Marketing Managers can expect to earn $60k - $120k + a 15 - 20% bonus.

Landing Your First Job

There is no defined entryway to a career in content marketing.

A degree in English, Journalism, Technical Writing, or a related field would provide an excellent foundation. Also, some experience as a blogger or managing social media pages are also useful.

Develop 'proof points' by creating a portfolio highlighting your writing and/or editorial capabilities.. Try to get some 'hands-on' experience by creating content for a website based on one of your passions, write a blog, or find a sponsor who needs their website content refreshed. These activities will enable you to have a robust content portfolio to show (and impress) prospective employers.

USER EXPERIENCE DESIGN

User Experience Design is a process used for designing digital products that best meet the needs of the customer. The goal is to create a 'user experience' that is useful, fast, easy, engaging, and intuitive for the customer when using the product. This was best defined by Apple's Chief Design Officer, Johnny Ives: "There is beauty when something works and works intuitively".

UX Designer

UX Designers are the chief architects of the digital product experience. Using Web UX as an example, they work to define a site experience that enables the customer to effortlessly achieve the goal of their web visit i.e. to find specific information, make a purchase, fill out a form, interact with a video, etc. UX Designers will design the overall architecture of the website, determining the role and purpose of each site section, the structure of each webpage, and the cross-site navigation.

UX Designers are digital strategists who involve customer (user) feedback in every phase of the product's development. They develop prototypes and wireframes and relentlessly collect hands-on feedback from the customer through multiple rounds of testing and iterations. With the overall user experience defined, the UX Designer then guides the work of the Interaction (UI) Designer.

Responsibilities (Website UX Designer)
· Lead the planning and execution of user research
· Interpret user feedback and make actionable recommendations for UX enhancements
· Create user journey maps, user stories, and personas
· Develop the information architecture and sitemaps

· Create prototypes and wireframes
· Conduct usability testing

Career Path

Job titles can vary widely across companies, but UX careers generally progress from UX Designer to UX Manager to UX Director.

Salaries

UX Design is a hot field but there is a wide range of salaries—as low as $50k at smaller companies to as high as $160k at large companies or agencies.

Success Factors

- The User-Centered Design
- Ethnographic research
- The Agile development processes
- Design software including Figma, Sketch, and Invision
- Understanding of HTML, CSS, and JavaScript

Landing Your First Job

Careers in both Interactive and User Experience Design require exceptional training. There are many courses available from universities and private online education platforms for a fee. I would recommend Bentley University's User Experience certification course since this

would provide you with excellent training (available online), and you'd receive your credentials from a highly reputable university. Also, consider 'boot camps' such as General Assembly.

I would also strongly suggest reaching out to UX Designers via LinkedIn or other platforms to ask for their guidance on breaking into the field.

UI Designer Responsibilities

Interaction design is about creating a 'language' between a

digital product and its user. Based on the experience defined by the UX Designer, the UI designer focuses on how the user (customer) interacts with the digital product. When you open your laptop, how do you turn it on? Where do you start to surf the internet? How do you access the photos you've uploaded? Now that I have made my online purchase, how do I 'check out'? etc. The interaction designer plans exactly how users interact online and then designs the digital 'interactions'.

The goal of UI is create a visual and interactive experience that makes it effortless and enjoyable for the user. For a website, the UI Designer designs the interactive elements of the site including how buttons, drop-down menus, sliders, video players, etc. 'look' (i.e., shapes, colors, sizes, text, etc.) to make it as effortless as possible to achieve the goal of their visit.

Web UI Responsibilities
· Collaborate with the UX Designer to define the web interaction and visual experience
· Execute visual design stages across all phases of website development
· Create interaction design that makes it effortless and seamless for the web visitor
· Create wireframes and user flows to articulate interaction and design ideas
· Establish style guides, design standards, guidelines, and best practices

Career Path
UI designers are typically 'individual contributor' roles but can progress to the UX Design career path noted above.

Salaries

UI Design is also a hot field where salaries can also range considerably—from $50k at smaller companies to as high as $120k at large companies or agencies.

Success Factors

UI Designers have deep knowledge of design principles including branding, typography, and color. They also have many of the same skills noted in UX Design including:
- The User-Centered Design process
- The Agile development process
- Design software including Figma, Sketch, and Invision
- Understanding of HTML, CSS, and JavaScript

Landing Your First Job

Interactive Design also requires exceptional training offered by private 'boot camps', as well as universities. There are many options. So do your homework to find the most reputable program that fits your budget. Also, reach out to UI Designers via LinkedIn or other platforms to ask for their guidance on breaking into the field. One 'watch out': beware of firms or individuals that charge fees for 'mentoring'.

Related Roles

Digital Producer

Overview

Digital producer roles can vary in scope depending on the company, but generally involve managing the creation and publishing of webpages, email marketing programs, digital ads, and 'digitizing' printed content.

Key Responsibilities

· Produce and publish web content updates in the content management system

· Oversee production of digital media including videos, online advertising, and email
· Design and build campaign web pages incorporating SEO and web accessibility
· Convert email design files to HTML using responsive email best practices
· Create automated e-mail marketing programs

· Communicate project status and timelines, ensuring all internal clients are updated on the delivery of digital campaigns.
· Coordinate with project directors to ensure that workflow, documentation, and design standards are being upheld.

Success Factors

· Enterprise content management system experience e.g., Adobe AEM, Sitecore.
· Experience building automated customer journeys in Marketing Cloud or similar email automation platform.
· Strong project management skills. Ability to multi-task.
· Ability to collaborate and build relationships across the organization.
· Excellent communication skills (written, oral, and internal stakeholder-facing).
· Proficient in HTML, CSS, multimedia, SEO, SEM, and other Internet technologies and best practices.

Career Path

Digital producers usually begin as 'Associates' and then progress to 'Producer' and then 'Sr. Producer'. The career path can lead to management of a team of digital producers, ultimately achieving the title of 'Head of Digital Production'.

Salaries

Salaries can vary significantly based on the size and location of the company. In some cases, the pay can be as

low as $40k, but entry-level roles at larger companies are between $50k and $65k. With a few years of experience, Digital producers can expect to earn $80k - $90k.

Job Outlook
The Bureau of Labor Statistics expects digital producer jobs to grow 5% per year between 2018 and 2028.

Landing Your First Job
If you don't have any digital production experience, consider building a portfolio by creating your own websites. Use free platforms such as Google Sites to create webpages on a topic of interest e.g. 'my snowboarding website'. Even better would be to volunteer or freelance for a local business or non-profit organization. There are also many certifications you can explore via Code Academy (https://www.codecademy.com/) and Coursera (https://www.coursera.org/). Look for certifications in basic web coding, content management systems (Adobe provides AEM certifications), marketing automation (Salesforce offers many), SEO, and web accessibility.

Digital Graphic Designer
Digital graphics are the visual images and designs that appear on a webpage, brand social media pages, mobile apps, prints, brochures, brand e-mails, digital ads, among others. The digital graphic designer determines which graphics should be created and how they should be presented to create a beautiful and powerful experience.

We've all seen web pages that are so cluttered and disorganized that it's impossible to focus. Great digital graphic designers find the right balance of content and 'white space' to make it easy to locate key information. They also know how to assemble photos, infographics, and videos in a way that 'commands' customer interaction.

Responsibilities

· Design a wide range of digital assets including email, social media, and website graphics as well as animation, video, and digital ads.
· Apply the latest design trends to enhance the brand image and customer experience across digital channels.

Career Path

Graphic Designers have terrific foundational skills to advance to more complex (and more lucrative) roles such as User Experience & Design and User Interface Design. However, this will require a fair amount of training, either as a trainee or through schooling. Graphic design is also a great field to 'be your own boss' and work as a contractor. Of course, this is only possible after getting at least a few years of experience under your belt by working for a company or agency.

Salaries

Expect to earn somewhere between $50k and $75k if working for a mid-large company or agency located in a larger city. Salaries can be rather low ($30k - $40k) if working for a smaller company or agency.

Job Outlook

The job outlook is very good given the proliferation of digital and social media channels.

Landing Your First Job

Creating a portfolio of your work from school or other activities is a great start. Hiring managers can easily see and assess your skills. I have personally hired graphic designers with no formal experience solely based on work they created at school or for their personal interests.

CONSUMER PROMOTION MANAGEMENT

Consumer Promotion Management plans and implements a wide spectrum of activities all geared to driving consumer trial and repeat purchases. This includes executing 'old school' tactics such as couponing , contests, and in-store sampling programs. However, digital media and technology have spurred an entirely new generation of highly engaging (and viral) promotional activities.

Consumer Promotion is a core function within consumer goods companies and is essential for acquiring new customers and retaining existing ones.

Consumer Promotion Manager

The Consumer Promotion Manager is assigned to a brand or group of brands, and leads the planning and implementation of all consumer promotion programs. They (usually) report to a Consumer Promotion Director but take overall business direction from the Brand Manager.

The Manager leads plans that either promote consumer 'trial' or 'retention'. Trial programs seek to obtain new brand users by inducing them with various offers to try the product—couponing, sampling, contest, etc.

Retention programs ensure that current customers keep buying the product. Customer Lifetime Value is a marketing principle that focuses on a minority of a brand's customers, the 'Most Valuable Customers' (MVCs). No matter the brand, only a small percentage of customers

are responsible for the majority of its profits. The consumer promotion manager works relentlessly to build this pool of MVCs while ensuring that current MVCs stay loyal to the brand.

Most of the implementation work is done by outside vendors—who distribute the coupons, manage the event or sampling program, etc. However, it is the Consumer Promotion Manager's job to hire them and coordinate their activities.

Responsibilities

- Lead the planning and execution of promotional programs to stimulate trial and ongoing consumer purchases.
- Create consumer promotion programs that support defined marketing objectives
- Conceptualize highly creative promotions that differentiate the brand
- Plan, execute, and measure promotional programs (discounts, samples, gifts, rebates, coupons, sweepstakes, and contests) via direct mail, inserts in newspapers, digital media, in-store displays, product endorsements, or other special events
- Present promotional plans to Marketing, Sales, and senior management.
- Recruit and manage external vendors supporting promotional programs.
- Leverage digital and social media as promotional channels
- Be the 'thought leader' for innovative and creative approaches to consumer promotion.

Success Factors

Effective consumer promotion managers are smart, creative, and highly energetic. They are passionate about finding new ways to 'connect with' and influence consumers. They are also highly 'detail oriented'- since their programs often reach tens of millions of customers, there is no margin for error. Consider the true story of one 'win a new car' promotion. The program offered a new car to the holder of the 'special key' that started a car at a local dealership. Unfortunately, some poor promotion manager allowed thousands of keys to be distributed to consumers—and each of them starting the car!

Skills Required
· Solid strategic thinking capabilities
· Strong creative thinking abilities
· Solid understanding of marketing strategy and brand positioning
· Superior project management skills and attention to detail
· Strong written and verbal communication skills

Competencies Required
· Strong decision-making skills
· Solid influencing skills
· Superior ability to multi-task and manage multiple priorities
· Solid analytical skills to assess program performance
· Strong collaboration capabilities

Pros/Cons
Pros

- It's both a 'strategic' and 'creative role'
- Your work influences the actions of millions of people
- There is always an opportunity to create 'something new'
- This role is somewhat less competitive than other marketing roles
- Solid employment prospects

Cons

- Often highly stressful
- Pay is good but not as good as in other marketing areas
- Can be long hours during key time periods
- Not a path to executive management

Typical Work Week
· Attend the Product Marketing launch plan meeting
· Meet with the promotion vendor to discuss the in-store

sampling program
· Present the holiday program couponing plan to the Brand Manager
· Receive a debrief from Market Research on brand loyalty results
· Lead team workshop to assess 'new promotion trends'
· Meet with Social Media Manager to review Facebook and Twitter promotional programs

Career Path

Consumer Promotion management is a highly specialized career and not a path to senior management. You will typically start as a Promotion Assistant, working for a Promotion Manager. You will move up to the Manager level after two or three years. After 5+ years as a Manager, the next (and usually final) rung on the ladder is Consumer Promotion Director. Of course, it is entirely possible to make a lateral move into Brand or Product Marketing if you're interested in long-term career potential.

Salaries

Consumer Promotion Managers can expect to earn $75k - $120k plus a 15 - 20% bonus at companies that have $1 billion or more in annual sales revenue.

Landing Your First Job

Promotion management is a very good entry-level job that does not require an MBA or Master's degree. But it can be highly competitive to land a role with a marquee company. The key to landing the first role is being able to articulate what attracts you to this field. Why do you like it? What do you know about this kind of work and why would you be a good fit? What are your favorite promotions, and which have influenced you to buy the brand?

You probably have had some 'promotional' experience in

your lifetime—any job that involved getting someone to 'try something new'. Find an experience or two from your past that might serve as a reference point for a promotional experience. And don't forget the ever-im

portant need to shine in 'self-promotion'. Besides your resume, think of other creative ways to promote yourself to the hiring manager. A great friend from Unilever landed his first job there by shipping his resume to the Promotion Director responsible for Promise Margarine in an empty tub of the product along with a note that read, 'I Promise to be the best promotion assistant you ever hired'. He was immediately called in for an interview and hired on the spot!

Related Careers

Shopper Marketing

Do shoppers who live in wealthy neighborhoods respond to retail promotions the same way as shoppers in less affluent ones? Do shoppers in Boston suburbs behave the same as those in Atlanta? Some things may be similar but many are not due to regional, cultural, economic, and other influences. Understanding and applying these insights to influence in-store sales is the role of the Shopper Marketer.

Shopper marketing was developed by fast-moving consumer goods companies (such as Procter & Gamble) to address marketing at a 'street level'—something their national consumer and trade promotion programs just cannot do. Shopper Marketing is about understanding local shopping dynamics and then planning and implementing retail marketing programs to increase brand sales. How do consumers plan their overall shopping? How do they navigate the supermarket or drug store aisles? What brands are in their consideration set as they shop a particular category? What in-store variables influence their selection of specific products? How sensitive are they to price discounts?

With these insights, the shopper marketer creates customized in-store programs to maximize brand sales. They might change the product assortment in the store based on local tastes or partner with a complementary brand to create an 'end aisle' display (e.g., a pasta sauce brand with a pasta brand). Shopper marketing programs also include in-store sampling as well as special events (e.g., in-store cooking classes or contests). The job offers many opportunities to creatively drive brand results.

The shopper marketer uses data to gain the customer insights that drive their programs. 'Scanner' data provides highly detailed information about what is purchased in a specific store, at what price, and through which promotions. The shopper marketer uses this data to relentlessly improve the product assortment, pricing, and promotional programs to maximize brand sales.

The Grocery Manufacturers Association published a study indicating that 70% of brand selections are made while at the store. So, it's no surprise that fast-moving consumer goods companies are investing significantly in Shopper Marketing. Done right, Shopper marketing can significantly impact sales. No wonder it is a growing field with a solid future.

Responsibilities
- Lead planning, execution, and measurement for shopper marketing strategies and tactics that meet or exceed established business goals.
- Plan and execute the calendar of promotional tactics including in-store media, trail-inducing promotional

programs, product sampling, direct mail, and event marketing.

- Develop a leading-edge understanding of the brand's consumers and their shopping needs and in-store purchasing behaviors.
- Strategically allocate the shopper marketing budget for optimal return-on-investment
- Hire and supervise third-party vendors in support of promotional programs
- Optimize the 'brand experience' at the point-of-sale

Typical Work Week

· Attend the launch plan meeting for a new product introduction
· Meet with the Brand Manager to plan next quarter's product assortment strategy
· Meet with the Consumer Promotion Manager to review the holiday program couponing plan
· Receive debrief from Market Research on Shopper Marketing study results.
· Analyze the results of last month's Walmart in-store program
· Finalize the special holiday trade promotion program

· Answer calls and e-mails from field sales reps

Career Path

Shopper marketing will continue to grow in stature, but your career will max out at middle management. That said, it's a terrific role to gain an unmatched understanding of the consumer and retail markets—solid foundations to move laterally into brand marketing, sales, and even consumer insight (market research) career paths.

Salaries

Shopper Marketers can expect to earn $75k - $125k plus a 20 - 25% bonus.

Pros/Cons

Pros

- It's an important job with significant responsibility and budget
- Excellent experience for a career in brand management or sales
- The job is one part 'corporate' and one part 'sales'
- The impact of your work is very measurable
- You are based in the field without day-to-day corporate oversight
- The job usually provides a decent work-life balance

Cons

- It's a very specialized role
- Balancing the needs of the retailer, the sales force and the business can be challenging
- There is constant 'tension' between driving sales and profit
- This is not a career path to executive management
- The pay is decent but not as good as a sales or brand marketing position

Success Factors

The shopper marketer needs a solid combination of 'street selling' and strategic thinking capabilities. An intuitive understanding of the deals, products, and in-store communication that trigger a purchase decision is the key ingredient to success. The shopper marketer also sits at the intersection of the brand, the sales force, and the customer. So, the ability to mediate their respective objectives to create 'win-win-win' outcomes is critical.

Skills

· Solid business planning and analytical aptitude
· Strong interpersonal relationship skills
· Strong understanding of the retail trade promotion planning process
· Solid understanding of consumer marketing activities

· Strong project management and prioritization skills
· Solid abilities as a 'creative problem solver'
· Strong attention to detail

Competencies
· Superior influencing skills
· Superior ability to multi-task and manage multiple priorities
· Strong collaboration capabilities
· Strong decision-making skills
· A passion for and deep understanding of the shopper

Landing Your First Job
A college degree in Marketing or Sales Administration combined with any kind of sales, consumer promotion, or retail experience is a great foundation. Begin by researching shopper marketing jobs on the career section of fast-moving consumer goods company websites

As you interview for entry-level positions you will need to demonstrate your ability to think from the shopper's point of view. What unplanned purchase did you make recently in a grocery or drug store? What factors (brand reputation, price, display placement, etc.) made you 'stop and look' and ultimately confirm your decision to buy? There is no 'right or wrong' answer to this question but this is the kind of thinking that will impress any prospective employer.

The Bottom Line
As a shopper marketer, you have a 'blank canvas' upon which to make your mark on the in-store brand experience. You'll have ample opportunity to show your 'strategic' and 'creative' sides. Your ability to find deep shopper insights and leverage to conceive and implement differentiating programs will be key to the success of your brand's sales as well as your career.

Merchandising (Store Experience) Manager

The term 'Merchandising Manager' is frequently used to describe a similar role to the shopper marketer at

clothing, electronics, retail, and other non-CPG companies. While these retail environments are vastly different, the same principles of driving profitable sales by understanding consumer in-store shopping dynamics hold true. Translating these insights into the right product assortment, pricing, and promotional programs is essential to the success of the retailer.

TRADE MARKETING MANAGEMENT

Trade marketing is an essential function for companies that sell 'indirectly'. This means products are initially sold to a company, who in turn sells to the final customer. For its product to reach a customer, a B2C company must first sell to retailer such as Walmart, while B2B companies must first sell to various intermediaries. Trade marketing tactics are vastly different within these industries, but the ultimate objective is the same —to induce your channel partner to stock and promote your products to the final buyer.

B2C marketing is divided into 'push' and 'pull' promotional activities. 'Pull' means those marketing activities seen by consumers outside of the retail environment to motivate them to 'pull' the product off the store shelf—mainly advertising and consumer promotion programs. 'Push' refers to programs designed to get retailers to 'push' the product to consumers at the point of sale—mainly through promotion incentives such as pricing discounts and special display programs. We'll review the roles of Trade Promotion Manager, Trade Merchandising Manager, and Shopper Marketer in this section.

B2B (business-to-business) companies often refer to this activity as Channel Marketing. Tech companies such as IBM sell hardware and software to an array of channel partners including software developers, IT system integrators, and other resellers. This requires dedicated marketing programs to induce these channel partners to

include the product as part of their offering to the end customer. Marketing programs are customized to offer the right set of products, pricing, and promotion incentives to the channel partner.

Trade Promotion Marketing Manager

As noted, this role is all about 'pushing' products at retail and requires having one foot in Sales and another foot in Marketing. Why is this Trade Promotion such an important role? Despite all the effort and expense to build a loyal customer base, the overwhelming majority of the time the consumer simply does not perceive significant differentiation between the top brands within any given category. The store shelf is THE decisive battleground, the moment of truth, for winning sales and market share.

B2C trade promotion focuses on the planning and implementation of price promotions (Temporary Price Reductions), special in-store placements (such as end-aisle displays), and special promotions (e.g., Buy One Get One Free). The trade promotion manager works on a 'national' or 'regional' basis and manages promotions for a specific product category (such as 'hair care') across multiple drugstores and supermarket retailers. They direct the flow of millions of dollars of the company's money to develop programs for retail partners that maximize sales velocity while still delivering acceptable profit margins. Promote the product too aggressively with a deeply discounted price, and the company loses money on each unit sold (not a good business practice, to say the least...).

Promote the product too conservatively and sales goals are not met (also not a good thing...).

The trade promotion manager sits in the real world 'hot-seat'— with consumers voting each day about his or her performance with their purchases.

Responsibilities

- Partner with Sales and Marketing to develop customer-specific strategies that integrate sales plans, product

plans, and marketing objectives.
- Have a deep understanding of the goals and needs of the retail account, the brand, and the customer.
- Develop account-specific short and long-term trade promotion business plans.
- Build strong, trusting 'partner-based' relationships with key retail account managers, the Salesforce, and the Marketing teams.
- Negotiate Win-Win outcomes for the retail account and the brand.
- Lead the planning for retail product assortment, merchandising, and trade promotions.
- Customize the product mix and shelf placement to maximize sales within each retail account.
- Develop the promotion and merchandising calendar for retail accounts and ensure alignment with consumer promotion, advertising, and other marketing activities.
- Ensure that trade programs work synergistically with the brand's advertising and consumer promotion 'pull' marketing programs.
- Lead trade promotion measurement and analysis and report results versus objectives to senior Sales and Marketing management.
- Analyze sales trends based on pricing and trade promotion to assess the overall revenue and profit impact.

Typical Work Week
· Attend the Product Marketing launch plan meeting
· Meet with the Brand Manager to plan next quarter's product assortment strategy
· Meet with Consumer Promotion Manager to review the holiday program couponing plan
· Have lunch with local market Sales Rep
· Receive a debrief from Market Research on the new Shopper Marketing study

· Analyze results of last month's Walmart program
· Finalize the special holiday trade promotion program
· Answer calls and e-mails from field sales reps
· Have dinner with field sales colleagues

Career Path

From my experience, trade promotion management is not a dedicated career path but serves as a valuable, but temporary career development 'stint'. Usually, high-potential sales reps are offered these roles as stepping-stones to future higher levels of management. The role will test their strategic and analytical skills, as well as their ability to effectively work within a 'corporate' environment. It's a good job to gain the 'big picture view' of the industry, and to work side-by-side with the brand marketing, market research, and consumer promotion

teams. This provides invaluable career development, and a deep understanding of how consumer marketing works at both the 'macro' and 'micro' levels.

Salaries

Trade Marketing Managers can expect to earn $80k - $130k + a 25 - 30% bonus at companies with $1 billion or more in annual sales revenue.

Pros/Cons

Pros

- It's an important job with significant responsibility and budget
- Excellent experience for a career in brand management or sales
- The job is one part 'corporate' and one part 'sales'
- The impact of your work is very measurable
- This can be a path to senior sales and marketing management
- There is usually a good work-life balance

Cons

- It's a very specialized and focused role
- Balancing the needs of the retailer, the sales force and the business can be challenging
- There is constant 'tension' between driving sales and profit
- The pay is good but usually not as good as a field sales position
- The constant analysis and reporting can be a grind.

Success Factors

The best Trade Promotion Managers are skilled salespeople with sharp 'strategic' instincts. Relationships matter greatly. The manager must build and maintain a strong rapport with retailer partners, as well as with the sales force. This means truly understanding their respective goals and being an advocate to achieve win-win outcomes. Sometimes these needs come in conflict with the expectations of the company or brand, and it's the Trade Promotion Manager's role to sort it out.

Skills

- Solid strategic planning and analytical skills.
- Excellent communication and interpersonal relationship skills.
- Strong understanding of the retail trade promotion planning process.
- A deep understanding of the shopper within the given category.
- Solid understanding of consumer marketing activities
- Strong project management and prioritization skills

Competencies

- Superior influencing skills
- Superior ability to multi-task and manage multiple priorities

- Strong collaboration capabilities
- Strong decision-making skills

Landing Your First Job

Trade promotion roles are not usually entry-level positions, although 'Assistant Merchandising' and 'Trade Analyst' roles are sometimes available. Virtually all trade promotion managers have solid experience as field sales reps or were recruited from the marketing ranks. My advice would be to first pursue an entry-level sales or sales analyst job and then seek a two-year assignment in trade marketing at a later point in your career.

The Bottom Line

Trade Promotion is one of the less glamorous jobs in marketing, However, gaining 2-3 years of experience will provide an unmatched understanding of the retail trade and will pay huge dividends in terms of future Product and Brand Management roles.

EVENT MARKETING MANAGEMENT

Event marketing is about the design and execution of in-person, and virtual events that exhibit and promote a product or a company. An 'event' can be a booth at a tradeshow, a huge 'Hollywood-like' production in a major arena, or a highly immersive virtual experience via remote technology. The COVID pandemic has radically altered the profession, expanding the landscape of event types which now include webinars, virtual roundtable discussions, podcast interviews, online summits, panels, and large virtual meetings.

Business-to-business companies frequently stage large events to promote their services and/or new product introductions. For many companies, event marketing is a core component of their marketing mix. Information Technology and Healthcare are two industries that rely heavily on these major gatherings to present their wares in the best possible light to the purchase decision-makers. The outcome of these events is often "make or break" activities for sales. Apple and Samsung invest millions in massive events to introduce their latest rounds of innovations. These events are attended by thousands of people including the investment community and the international news media and stock prices rise and fall as the new line-up is unveiled.

Event Manager
Similar Titles: Virtual Event Manager

Event Managers are responsible for the planning, execution, and measurement of a variety of customer-facing live events. These include industry trade shows (such as CES, the annual Consumer Electronics Show in Las Vegas), as well as company-specific events and traveling 'roadshows' that are exclusive to the company's products.

Activities can include managing all or some of the aspects of an event including:
- finding the event location (hotel, resort, or other venues)
- determining the event agenda
- booking speakers and entertainment
- arranging for food & and beverage
- coordinating registration
- arranging stage lighting and audio-visual gear

The goal of the event manager is to make every program a truly exciting and memorable one while ensuring that everything 'runs smoothly'. The event manager must also know how to measure if the event was a success based on feedback from the customer as well as event participants.

Responsibilities
- Lead planning for all customer tradeshows, exhibits, and roadshows as well as important internal company events.
- Lead event registration logistics.
- Coordinate all event logistics activities including venue management, food & beverage, speaker and staging coordination, and audio-visual requirements.
- Ensure that event themes, signage, and graphics support the overall marketing objectives and brand positioning.
- Ideate and collaborate with the Brand or Corporate marketing teams to identify creative and engaging event themes.
- Establish quantifiable objectives for the event.
- Manage the event budget and negotiations with third-party vendors.
- Recruit, train, and supervise event/booth staff and third-party vendors.
- Be a 'thought leader' in the latest trends and technologies

in event marketing.

Typical Work Week

· Receive updates from Marketing on the new product launch plans

· Meet with the Sales Director to finalize the Annual Sales meeting invitation list

· Review the 'satisfaction survey' results from last week's 'loyal customer' event

· Meet with a virtual technology vendor to review new event registration and event

  management tools

· Review proposals from potential vendors for next year's trade show

· Finalize a report to the Event Director on last quarter's customer roadshow

· Review new webcasting platform options with the IT team

· Meet with an audio-visual vendor for the annual investor conference

· Leave for the airport to scout potential resorts for the Annual Sales Meeting

Career Path

Event marketing is a highly specialized career and does not provide a path to senior management. You will likely start as an Assistant Event Manager and support one specific event activity at any given time. You will work your way up to Event Manager after two to three years and manage the planning and execution of multiple events throughout the year. Career progression is typically capped as an Event Director, leading event marketing activities across the entire company.

Despite the rise of digital technologies, face-to-face meetings will remain an essential component of the marketing mix for many marketers. Event Marketing provides a solid career option that is dynamic and rewarding. There are also ample opportunities to move from the 'client side' to event management agencies and vendors.

Salaries

Event Managers can expect to earn $70k - $120k plus a 15 - 20% bonus at companies with $1 billion or more in annual sales revenue.

Success Factors

Great event marketers are tireless perfectionists and are never satisfied with just putting on a 'good' event. They see every event as a new challenge to run an even smoother program and to deliver an even higher level of attendee satisfaction. The event marketer must understand the 'big picture' and consider how overall business goals can be supported by the event. Is the business goal to introduce a new product, reward current loyal customers, or communicate news to the press? What should the 'tone & manner' of the event be—formal? fun? And how is the company's brand image best represented through the event presentation?

Above all, the Event Manager must have superior organization and 'multi-tasking' skills, and be able to effectively manage the wide variety of third-party vendors required to support all aspects of the event.

Skills
· Superior project management skills
· Deep understanding of Microsoft Teams, Zoom Meetings/ Webinars
· Strong interpersonal relationship skills
· Solid understanding of marketing strategy
· Solid abilities as a 'creative problem solver'
· Superior attention to detail
· Superior communication and interpersonal skills

· Strong negotiating skills

Competencies
· Solid leadership skills
· Solid influencing skills

· Superior ability to multi-task and manage multiple priorities
· Superior ability to work effectively under tight timelines in a fast-paced environment
· Strong collaboration capabilities
· Strong decision-making skills

Pros/Cons
Pros
- An exciting and creative job
- The job is one part 'corporate', one part 'show business
- The results of your work are experienced by many
- Frequent travel, often to nice locations
- Good job stability

Cons
- It's a very specialized role
- The job can be highly stressful due to the unpredictability of live events
- It's not a career path to executive management
- Good pay but on the lower end of the marketing pay scale
- Some travel will likely require weekends away from home

Landing Your First Job
Employers will be looking for smart candidates with a high degree of passion for the profession who have demonstrated exceptional organizational and interpersonal skills. They will also be looking for candidates with a high 'energy level' that works well under extreme pressure and tight timelines.

You can easily get event management experience by

volunteering your time to work at a school function or a local community or non-profit event. After helping out a few times, you should be able to raise your hand to lead the end-to-end planning and execution of an entire event.

The Bottom Line

This is a dynamic career option that has one foot in 'show business' and the other in marketing. Events are "real-time" with little margin for error in their planning and implementation. And the bar keeps getting raised in terms of the quality and "wow factor" expected by attendees. This career path can indeed be a high-pressure one but also one filled with significant opportunities for creativity with ample ability to make a significant impact on the business.

MARKETING TECHNOLOGY MANAGEMENT

Similar Titles: Marketing Platform Manager, Marketing Technology Product Manager

Marketing technology management is increasingly in demand as companies accelerate their digital transformation. Marketing Technology Managers sit at the intersection of Marketing and IT. They translate marketing objectives into marketing technology requirements which then guide the purchasing and implementation of the technology.

Marketing technology management roles lead planning and operations for one or more of the following platforms:
- Marketing Automation/e-mail Marketing platform
- Website Content Management platform (SMS)
- Marketing Productivity tools e.g. project management and campaign workflow
- Digital Asset Management platform (DAM)
- Customer Data Platform (CDP)
- E-Commerce platform

Responsibilities

• Represent the needs of the Marketing organization for marketing technology.

• Collaborate with Marketing to develop marketing technology business requirements based on overall marketing goals.

• Translate marketing business requirements into 'user stories', articulating end-user technology needs.

• Partner with the IT team to execute the product vision.

• Monitor marketing technology product performance and continuously make improvements for a better product experience.

• Develop the marketing technology product development

roadmap and report progress to internal stakeholders.

• Serve as a 'thought leader' and recommend emerging marketing technologies relevant to the business.

Career Path

Marketing technology managers can progress to roles with responsibility for additional elements of the marketing technology stack, thus advancing to Sr. Technology Managers and Technology Directors.

Job Outlook & Salaries

The job outlook is very promising and demand for these roles is very likely to grow in the years ahead. These are high-paying roles ranging from $70k to $135k for managers and up to $200k for directors.

• Strong project management skills.

• Excellent collaboration and communication skills.

• Some knowledge of digital design and engineering.

Landing Your First Job

Marketing technology manager jobs are not entry-level and require at least 2 years of experience as a Project Manager, Marketing Manager, CRM Manager, or Data Manager.

The following section discusses some of the hottest jobs in marketing today including:

- Marketing Analyst
- Data Scientist
- Related Careers

Marketing Analytics and Data Science

In the marketing world, 'data' generally refers to the information a company and/or brand has about its customers, sales, pricing, marketing investment, and campaign performance. Data is an essential asset and can serve as a major source of competitive advantage if properly managed, analyzed, and interpreted.

The analysis of data guides companies to make smarter and more informed business decisions:

- who are our best customers?
- how can we keep customersloyal?
- what other products do customers buy when buying my brand?
- which campaign tactics should we invest more in, and where should we invest less?
- what are the key trends in the market and how can the brand take advantage of them?

Marketing data analysts and data scientists answer these, and many more critical questions using a variety of methods to gain unique and forward-looking views of the market, consumers, and business performance.

While both roles have the same overall responsibility, they differ in terms of the depth and complexity of the analytics applied.

Marketing data analysts work in the 'Here and Now'. They

analyze and interpret existing data to explain current campaign performance and identify basic customer and market trends. This includes such work as interpreting which advertising creative and media is proving the best 'bang for the buck', as well as evaluating website 'click-stream' data to understand online customer behavior.

Marketing data scientists work in the 'Future'. They design new ways to process and model data to predict likely future outcomes, thus providing the business with the next best thing to a 'crystal ball'. This includes providing foresight as to which customers are most at risk of switching to the competitor's brand, and which customer segments have the greatest potential for future revenue growth? How large will the market be in five years from now?

DIGITAL MARKETING ANALYST

Annual spending on digital ads, social media, and paid search is well over $100 billion and continues to grow at double-digit rates. Digital is no longer just an experiment; it's a big investment and marketers demand optimal returns on their investment. The digital marketing analyst is paid to find and report timely insights from customer, market, and campaign data to maximize campaign performance.

The work of the analyst starts with understanding the overall digital objectives, and then structuring a measurement plan against them. An essential role of the analyst is to define what 'success' looks like for the program at hand. How many web visitors should be expected based on the investment? What's the target goal for the digital ad click-thru rate? How many site visitors should we expect to convert to a sale? What's the e-mail open rate target? etc.

A major advantage of digital marketing is that many results are available in real-time enabling 'winning' and 'losing' program features to be quickly identified. 'A/B' and 'multivariate' testing are used to test different 'variables' to optimize program performance—which landing page design best drives sales conversion? Does photo A or photo B achieve the highest click-thru rate? Which social media post is driving the most content sharing? The analyst relentlessly seeks to optimize program performance by 'Testing-Learning-Optimizing-Repeating'.

Responsibilities

- Develop the analytics plan to drive insightful and actionable digital marketing campaign performance.
- Define key performance indicators and build reporting dashboards that will allow marketing to rapidly

improve campaign impact and efficiency.
- Create and implement the marketing campaign data tracking and tagging framework.
- Design and maintain customer and campaign performance databases ensuring data quality and integrity.
- Work cross-functionally to translate business needs into analytics solutions— including data integration, data warehousing, QA reporting, and testing.
- Improve data quality by leveraging 1st party, 2nd party, and 3rd party data
- Design and implement testing and optimization programs including A/B testing, multivariate, and marketing mix analysis.

Typical Work Week

· Meet with the marketing team to review the new digital campaign plan.

· Present updated marketing dashboard to Marketing VP

· Design the A/B test to analyze alternative digital advertising creative

· Assess the performance of digital versus offline channels (ITV, outdoor, newspapers, etc.)

· Define key performance indicators for the new product campaign launch

· Conduct quality assurance check of data tagging for new media channels

· Meet with an analytics vendor to review new AI tools

Career Path and Salaries

Entry-level positions are usually not offered at large companies, but given the huge increase in demand for analytics, some companies do have internship programs. With some analytics experience (Landing Your First Job) your career would begin as an 'Analyst'(or 'Digital Analyst' and then progress to 'Senior

Analyst'. Management roles would come next with Associate Director (3 – 5 years of experience) and finally a Director position (10+ years of experience). Keep in mind that these roles also serve as springboards to the more advanced (and lucrative) world of Data Science (summarized in this section).

Analysts and Sr. Analysts earn anywhere between $70k - $140k depending on the industry, the size of the company, and the overall investment in marketing campaigns.

Job Outlook

The world runs on data. Marketing-driven companies need analytic experts to make sense of it so they can make smarter business decisions. The pandemic has intensified investment in digital transformation and hiring for these roles can be expected to increase substantially.

Pros/Cons

Pros

- It's a critical role that greatly contributes to company performance.
- You gain deep exposure to understanding the industry, the company, and the brand.
- The role is thought-provoking and constantly pushes new boundaries of learning.
- You will be the 'smartest one in the room' and be highly respected by your colleagues.
- The results of your work ultimately impact what millions of consumers experience.
- Excellent job stability with high pay.

Cons

- It's a very specialized role
- It's not a career path to executive management
- Offers fewer moments of collaboration with your colleagues

Skills
· Background in math and statistics
· Analytic and critical thinking mindset
· Deep understanding of applied statistics
· Strong quantitative skills
· Strong writing and presentation skills
· Strong project management skills
· Deep understanding of digital marketing channels, analytic tools and processes
· Qualitative and quantitative analysis research skills

Competencies
· A passion for transforming data into 'knowledge'
· Comfortable working in complex and sometimes ambiguous areas
· Ability to collaborate across the organization
· Relentless 'curiosity in data'

Landing Your First Job
If you believe this is the right career path for you, investigate pursuing a master's degree in data Analytics (usually a one-year program). If this option is not feasible, look into Google's Data Analytics Professional Certificate. Some companies do offer internships for those with a solid understanding of research methods and statistics.

Also consider taking on a volunteer job to analyze the website, search, and email marketing program of a non-profit organization or your school. This would provide some hands-on practical experience that would be of interest to many hiring managers.

Also, I'd strongly recommend reaching out to your network (alumni, LinkedIn connections, etc.) to learn how they entered the Data Analytics field. Also, become familiar with the Digital

Analytics Association and the wealth of information available on their website. https://www.digitalanalyticsassociation.org/Files/Education/DAA_Career_Guide_2019.pdf

The Bottom Line

Digital analytics offers an excellent career opportunity for those with a love of numbers. The pay is great, and the job stability is as 'good as it gets'. For those of you with strong quantitative skills, digital savviness, and an insatiable desire to 'get inside the head' of the customer this is a great career option with serious demand and growth potential.

Data Scientist

Marketing Data Scientists work in the 'Future' by designing new ways to process and model data to predict likely future outcomes. They apply analytical, mathematical, and computer science skills to extract meaning from data and find patterns to solve and predict the most complex business questions.

In many ways, this field is still in its infancy since the explosion of digital and associated data is opening vast new opportunities for advanced analytics, artificial intelligence, and machine learning. Demand for this role has increased dramatically since every business wants its version of a 'crystal ball' and 'trend spotter'.

Responsibilities
• Analyze customer data to create new hypotheses about user behavior and campaign performance.
• Lead the process to process multiple streams of large datasets to perform predictive analytics.
• Develop the data strategy and identify new data sources that can be mined insights.
• Design algorithms and models to mine multiple and disparate 'big data' sources.

• Analyze data for trends and patterns and Interpret data that address specific business challenges or opportunities.
• Clearly summarize and report analytic solutions to key business stakeholders.
• Apply modern analytic tools and write code to synthesize complex data

Career Path and Salaries

Compensation is excellent with average annual salaries ranging from $100k - $180k. Data Scientists can progress to more senior roles including data architect and data engineer.

Job Outlook

There is perhaps no better field for future job growth. The U.S. Government's Occupational Outlook Handbook projects a 36% increase in these roles between 2021 and 2031—over 7 times the average job growth rate!

Success Factors

- Expertise in coding for analysis data extraction (SQL, R, Python, Pandas)
• Experience with data processing frameworks like Hadoop, Scalding, Spark, Storm, Cassandra, and Kafka (for advanced positions)
• In-depth experience with data science, engineering, and analysis

Job Requirements

• Advanced degree in statistics, applied mathematics, or related fields is usually
  required
• Heavy coding experience (e.g., Python, object-oriented

programming)
• Machine learning – Python, object-oriented programming, and predictive modeling
• Proficiency with data mining, mathematics, and statistical analysis

The Bottom Line

If you are strong analytically and enjoy uncovering insights hidden in reams of data, you should certainly explore data science as a career. You will need some post-undergraduate training in statistics and related programming languages. And while this is a behind-the-scenes role, you will enjoy great pay, high job security, and be a highly respected contributor to your company.

RELATED ROLES

Marketing Data Manager

Similar titles: Customer Data Manager

Customer and campaign data are considered valuable company 'assets'. Quality data is essential to optimize marketing campaign performance. The marketing data manager supports the marketing organization by developing a robust and accurate database of customer information. These data provide marketers with unique insights that power highly segmented, targeted, and thus impactful marketing programs.

Key activities of the marketing data manager include importing, 'cleaning', and building targeted customer lists as well as applying the SQL programming language to store, configure, and extract data from the database to enable automated and personalized marketing campaigns.

Web Analytics Manager

Web Analytics Manager jobs typically exist in companies where the website is the primary digital channel. The objective of the role is to garner insights from website data so visitors have a great site experience and so the site can better support the company's or brand's marketing objectives. The Web Analytics Manager will analyze the behavior of site visitors—what pages, videos, links, etc. did they interact with on the site? What path do they navigate as they move from webpage to webpage?

Which web pages and content were most viewed, or most ignored?

Ultimately this role is about 'customer satisfaction' by helping customers easily find the information they are looking for, and once they find it, ensuring that it meets their needs. This role is increasingly morphing into the more relevant digital marketing analyst one as companies expand their digital 'footprint'.

Social Media Analyst

Smart marketers want smart insights to optimize the return on their social media investment. The social media analyst collects and interprets data about social media visitors to support this objective.

To do this, the social media analyst asks questions – MANY questions......Who is our social media audience? What type of content do they engage with? What motivates them to post, 'like', or 'tweet'? What programs are driving the most conversations? What content is most shared by brand fans on their social networks?

The Analyst is also responsible for setting up and monitoring the 'Social Listening' program to learn what consumers saying about the company, and to identify new cultural trends.

The social media analyst is an important role that 'looks under the hood' of this highly influential form of media. As such, their impact on the business can be very significant.

VI. FINAL THOUGHTS

Building off the last chapter, it's really important to think through many things as you 'point the compass' for your first job in marketing. The more honest you are with yourself now, the more the compass will be pointed in the right direction, minimizing any 'rethinking' about what you really want to do in the future.

Start by thinking about your passion and interests. Overlay on top of this your key strengths and differentiating talents. Factor in your tolerance for 'stress' and the scope of responsibilities. And then adjust for career growth and earnings potential. And 'presto' you have found the perfect marketing career. If only it were that simple.....

You will need to consider many factors to make the right career choice. Hopefully, this book has provided you with some clarity about the broad and complex landscape called 'marketing' and which career options might be best suited for you. My career has had its ups and downs but there has certainly been much more 'good' than 'bad'. I'd do it all over again. So, give it a good 'think' and keep me posted on your progress!